Clinical Natural Language Processing Workshop (ClinicalNLP 2016)

Osaka, Japan
11 December 2016

ISBN: 978-1-5108-3322-7

Preface

This volume contains papers from the Workshop on Clinical Natural Language Processing (ClinicalNLP).

Clinical text offers unique challenges that differentiate it both from open-domain data and from other types of text in the biomedical domain. Narrative clinical notes are written by experts for other experts, while also intended to serve as a legal record. Clinical jargon, non-standard document strucuture, privacy and security concerns all present special challenges for natural language systems. The workshop's goal is to attract more quality NLP researchers to the clinical domain, and thereby to allow us as a community to contribute more to the advancement of critical clinical research.

Organizers

Anna Rumshisky

Kirk Roberts

Steven Bethard

Tristan Naumann

Program Committee

Sabine Bergler

Kevin Cohen

Dina Demner-Fushman

Dmitriy Dligach

Oladimeji Farri

Michele Filannino

Nazli Goharian

Cyril Grouin

Sanda Harabagiu

Sadid Hasan

Lynette Hirschman

Guergana Savova

Hongfang Liu

Stephane Meystre

Timothy Miller

Marie-Francine Moens

Danielle Mowery

Ted Pedersen

Amber Stubbs

Sumithra Velupillai

Ben Wellner

Jenna Wiens

Stephen Wu

Hua Xu

Pierre Zweigenbaum

Table of Contents

Conference Program

Sunday, December 11, 2016

09:00–09:30   ***Introductory Remarks***

09:30–10:30   *Invited Talk*
Tim Baldwin

10:30–10:45   **Coffee Break**

10:45–11:30   **Short Talks**

10:45–11:00   *The impact of simple feature engineering in multilingual medical NER*
Rebecka Weegar, Arantza Casillas, Arantza Diaz de Ilarraza, Maite Oronoz, Alicia Pérez and Koldo Gojenola

11:00–11:15   *Bidirectional LSTM-CRF for Clinical Concept Extraction*
Raghavendra Chalapathy, Ehsan Zare Borzeshi and Massimo Piccardi

11:15–11:30   *MedNLPDoc: Japanese Shared Task for Clinical NLP*
Eiji Aramaki, Yoshinobu Kano, Tomoko Ohkuma and Mizuki Morita

11:30–12:15   **Best Student Paper Award Session**

11:30–11:45   *Feature-Augmented Neural Networks for Patient Note De-identification*
Ji Young Lee, Franck Dernoncourt, Ozlem Uzuner and Peter Szolovits

11:45–12:05   *Semi-supervised Clustering of Medical Text*
Pracheta Sahoo, Asif Ekbal, Sriparna Saha, Diego Molla and Kaushik Nandan

12:15–14:00   Lunch

14:00–15:00   Long Talks

14:00–14:20   *Deep Learning Architecture for Patient Data De-identification in Clinical Records*
Shweta Yadav, Asif Ekbal, Sriparna Saha and Pushpak Bhattacharyya

14:20–14:40   *Neural Clinical Paraphrase Generation with Attention*
Sadid A. Hasan, Bo Liu, Joey Liu, Ashequl Qadir, Kathy Lee, Vivek Datla, Aaditya Prakash and Oladimeji Farri

14:40–15:00   *Assessing the Corpus Size vs. Similarity Trade-off for Word Embeddings in Clinical NLP*
Kirk Roberts

15:00–15:45   Poster Session

15:00–15:45   *Inference of ICD Codes from Japanese Medical Records by Searching Disease Names*
Masahito Sakishita and Yoshinobu Kano

15:00–15:45   *A fine-grained corpus annotation schema of German nephrology records*
Roland Roller, Hans Uszkoreit, Feiyu Xu, Laura Seiffe, Michael Mikhailov, Oliver Staeck, Klemens Budde, Fabian Halleck and Danilo Schmidt

15:00–15:45   *Detecting Japanese Patients with Alzheimer's Disease based on Word Category Frequencies*
Daisaku Shibata, Shoko Wakamiya, Ayae Kinoshita and Eiji Aramaki

15:00–15:45   *Prediction of Key Patient Outcome from Sentence and Word of Medical Text Records*
Takanori Yamashita, Yoshifumi Wakata, Hidehisa Soejima, Naoki Nakashima and Sachio Hirokawa

15:00–15:45   *Unsupervised Abbreviation Detection in Clinical Narratives*
Markus Kreuzthaler, Michel Oleynik, Alexander Avian and Stefan Schulz

15:00–15:45   *Automated Anonymization as Spelling Variant Detection*
Steven Kester Yuwono, Hwee Tou Ng and Kee Yuan Ngiam

The impact of simple feature engineering in multilingual medical NER

R. Weegar†, A. Casillas‡, A. Diaz de Ilarraza‡, M. Oronoz‡, A. Pérez‡, K. Gojenola‡
†Clinical Text Mining Group, DSV, Stockholm University
‡IXA NLP Group, University of the Basque Country (UPV-EHU)
`koldo.gojenola@ehu.es`

Abstract

The goal of this paper is to examine the impact of simple feature engineering mechanisms before applying more sophisticated techniques to the task of medical NER. Sometimes papers using scientifically sound techniques present raw baselines that could be improved adding simple and cheap features. This work focuses on entity recognition for the clinical domain for three languages: English, Swedish and Spanish. The task is tackled using simple features, starting from the window size, capitalization, prefixes, and moving to POS and semantic tags. This work demonstrates that a simple initial step of feature engineering can improve the baseline results significantly. Hence, the contributions of this paper are: first, a short list of guidelines well supported with experimental results on three languages and, second, a detailed description of the relevance of these features for medical NER.

1 Introduction

Named Entity Recognition (NER), such as the recognition of person names, organizations, locations or medical entities, has become a crucial task in any Natural Language Processing (NLP) application, as a first step to other types of processing as, for example, Relation Extraction (Oronoz et al., 2015). Several tools have been developed for this task, such as CRF++ (Kudo, 2013), SVM (Kudo and Matsumoto, 2001) or Perceptron (Collins, 2002). Using these tools, and training them with a set of annotated data, many people can obtain a NER system easily and apply it to the respective domain. In this paper the experiments will be performed with clinical texts, on the recognition of Medical entities such as disorder or drug brand names. The basic NER models make use of a sequence of *(word form, features, tag)* elements for training. For inference, the system will give the tag sequence with the highest score given a new text. Each model is defined by a set of features, taken from the surroundings of each word to be tagged, usually by means of a sequential tagging approach.

Many techniques have been developed in order to improve the NER results, such as the incorporation of additional information, in the form of lemmatization, POS tagging, dictionaries and ontologies (IHTSDO, 2016), or the inclusion of knowledge acquired by unsupervised techniques like Brown clusters (Brown et al., 1992; Clark, 2003), word2vec neural models (Agerri and Rigau, 2016) or deep neural network architectures (dos Santos and Guimarães, 2015) that yielded significant improvements.

However, this availability of tools and techniques has led to using only a limited set of predefined or standard models that were successful for a prototypical NER task, without any kind of time-consuming adjusting (Pradhan et al., 2014). Moreover, as most published papers center on novel techniques (Ratinov and Roth, 2009; Turian et al., 2010), sometimes less effort is devoted to data analysis or to filtering and tuning the models. Researchers rarely give the full details of feature engineering and they often present their best configurations, or otherwise they only study the impact of one or two specific types of feature. However, the benefits of sophisticated techniques would be better highlighted taking a stronger baseline as departure. In this sense, this paper may be useful to researchers that are new to the field of medical NER, showing the impact of simple feature engineering on medical texts in three languages.

As an example, looking at the systems presented at the Semeval 2014 Shared Task 7 on English Medical texts (Pradhan et al., 2014), we see that most of the system descriptions do not give a precise

1

overview of the contribution of the simplest feature types (Ramanan et al., 2014; Leal et al., 2014; Kate, 2014; Attardi et al., 2014) and they give at most a list of the used features, but without a detailed account of each's performance. For example, while Attardi et al. (2014) describe word shape features, they do not describe the window of words used, while Parikh et al. (2014) use a window of three words ([-2,0]).

There exist several available systems for English, as cTAKES (Savova et al., 2010), which was used by some of the participants at Semeval 2014 or cLiner (Boag et al., 2010). However, for other types of languages, there is a scarcity of resources and information about the usefulness of the available features.

We will experiment the effect of using simple features on medical NER, giving a measure of the improvements that can be achieved without resorting to more sophisticated types of information. Although most of these techniques have been previously applied in many works (Pradhan et al., 2014), we think that their effectiveness has not always been clearly evaluated, and they are briefly described as a preprocessing step before applying other, more complex, techniques. The main contribution of this paper will be a thorough examination of simple features for the recognition of entities in the medical domain. To give a better account of the generalization across different languages, we will perform our experiments on English, Spanish and Swedish, hoping that these results will be useful for many researchers and will help them to follow the principle of doing the easy things first, before resorting to more complex models.

2 Experimental Setup

We will perform a set of experiments using different types of features, starting from the most basic type of information, the word form itself and its derivatives, and continuing with basic language processing tools as lemmatization, POS tagging and medical dictionaries and ontologies: **Phase 1:** using only word forms (plus lower-casing); **Phase 2:** using prefixes and suffixes of different length. For example, the four letter suffix *-itis* indicates an inflamatory disease, as in meningitis or bronchitis; **Phase 3:** using different patterns of capitalization of word forms (word starts with a letter, all letters are capitalized, or different types of numbers); **Phase 4:** using lemmas; **Phase 5:** using POS tags. **Phase 6:** using Snomed-CT tags.

With the objective of establishing measures of the contribution of several features corresponding to simple types of information to medical NER, we will examine three languages:

- **English (EN)** We will use data from the SemEval-2014 Task 7 Analysis of Clinical Text Shared Task ShARe[1]. This corpus comprises annotations of disease entities (9,694 instances) over de-identified clinical reports from a US intensive care department (version 2.5 of the MIMIC II database)
- **Spanish (SP)** The Spanish EHRs consist of patient records collected during 2008-2012 at the Galdakao-Usansolo Hospital leading to 141,800 documents, 52 million word-forms (Oronoz et al., 2015). The entire corpus was provided after anonymization, signing confidentiality agreements and passing the corresponding ethical committees. From this set of raw clinical text, a subset of 121 texts was randomly selected for manual annotation (3,362 instances of diseases and 1,406 drugs).
- **Swedish (SW)** The Swedish clinical text[2] origins from patient records from over 500 different clinical units at Karolinska University Hospital. The texts were collected during 2009-2010 and are stored in HEALTH BANK (Dalianis et al., 2015). For this study, a supervised corpora was created, annotated with medical entities (4,000 entities corresponding to body parts, disorders and findings).

Regarding the English corpus, we only had access to the train and development sets, because the test set was not public. This is not a problem, because from our experiments on the Semeval Shared Task datasets, the results on the test set increased by about 2 percent points (Pradhan et al., 2014), as using the train and development sets for training compensates the effect of evaluating on the unseen test set. For that reason, we will use the train set for training and will evaluate on the development set.

For the experiments, we will use our own implementation of the averaged structured perceptron (Freund and Schapire, 1999; Collins, 2002), a state of the art tagging model that relies on Viterbi decoding of training examples combined with simple additive updates. The algorithm is competitive to maximum-entropy taggers or CRFs (Collins, 2002). For each experiment, we trained 25 iterations on different feature templates. Although not reported in this work, similar experiments have also been performed

---

[1]http://share.healthnlp.org
[2]This research was approved by the Regional Ethical Review Board in Stockholm, permission number 2014/1882-31/5

Perceptron. Phase 1 (word forms)				
Features	**Model**	**EN**	**SP**	**SW**
Window	wf(-2, +2)	**51.20**	51.07	55.94
size	wf(-2, +1)	49.20	52.46	56.09
(word	wf(-2, 0)	46.80	50.70	55.61
unigrams)	wf(-1, +1)	47.70	**52.49**	57.16
	wf(-1, 0)	40.10	50.18	**58.47**
Window	wf(-2, +2)	53.30	57.20	57.98
size	wf(-2, +1)	**54.30**	**57.74**	57.84
(lowercase	wf(-2, 0)	52.20	54.81	58.71
word	wf(-1, +1)	49.80	56.37	58.98
unigrams)	wf(-1, 0)	47.70	55.01	**60.44**

Table 1: Results changing the window size and capitalization of words (wf(i, j) = unigram features of words in a window from i to j).

Perceptron. Phase 2 (prefixes and affixes)				
Features	**Model**	**EN**	**SP**	**SW**
Adding	p2 + s2	59.40	60.74	62.27
prefixes/	p3 + s3	60.40	61.75	64.23
suffixes	p4 + s4	59.90	60.73	64.50
	p23 + s23	60.40	**63.27**	63.74
	p34 + s34	60.40	61.82	65.34
	p234 + s234	**60.50**	62.10	**66.36**
Adding	p2 + s2	59.10	62.13	62.59
prefixes/	p3 + s3	60.50	63.43	64.69
suffixes	p4 + s4	60.30	63.68	64.78
(lowercase)	p23 + s23	60.30	64.94	64.45
	p34 + s34	59.60	64.09	64.51
	p234 + s234	**61.00**	**65.23**	66.07

Table 2: Results adding prefixes and suffixes of word forms, using the best model of phase 1 as baseline. ($pN_1N_2...N_k$ = prefix of size N_1, N_2, ... N_k for the current word).

Perceptron. Phase 3 (capitalization and numbers)			
Model	**EN**	**SP**	**SW**
(1) all capital letters	60.30	65.99	**66.66**
(2) starts with capital letter	61.00	65.88	65.74
(3) number types	61.00	65.85	66.02
(4) mixed letters and numbers	60.10	64.59	65.68
(5) = (1) + (2)	**61.80**	66.04	65.72
(6) = (1) + (3)	60.20	**66.22**	66.02
(7) = (2) + (3)	60.90	65.34	66.06
(8) = (1) + (2) + (3)	61.20	65.86	65.45

Table 3: Results adding capitalization and numbers to the best model of phase 2.

Perceptron. Phase 4 (lemmas)				
Features	**Model**	**EN**	**SP**	**SW**
Window	lem(0)	61.40	65.82	66.12
size	lem(-1, +1)	**62.10**	66.13	65.31
	lem(-2, +2)	60.00	65.67	65.74

Table 4: Results adding features based on lemmas (on the best model of phase 3) (lem(i, j) = unigram features of lemmas in a window from i to j).

with SVM and CRFs, obtaining results comparable but slightly lower than with the Perceptron. For English and Spanish, we used FreelingMed for lemmatization, POS tagging, and annotating Snomed CT concepts (Oronoz et al., 2013). For Swedish, we used Stagger (Östling, 2013). The experiments were tested following a greedy approach, taking at each phase the best model in the previous phase as a baseline. This approach can be debatable, as it could happen that the knowledge used in phase $x+1$ could not be useful when applied with the best model in phase x, but perhaps it produced improvements at phases earlier than x. We have also experimented the effect of applying each set of features independently, but our aim is to get an account of the benefits obtained by applying a simple yet coherent approach (from the simplest to more elaborated experiments), and we leave out of the scope of this work the development of more time-consuming tests, such as grid search.

3   Results and Discussion

Table 1 shows the results (F-measure) with different values of the window size (WS). There is no use on trying a single WS for all the languages as it has different impacts on different languages. Note that lower-casing improved the results considerably for all three languages, specially for Spanish. We hypothesize that this can be due to the informal writing used in the Spanish medical reports, characterized by big differences in writing style and non-consistent use of casing (either lowercase, uppercase or mixed). The use of prefix/suffixes in Phase 2 (see Table 2) helps significantly for all the languages with respect to the best results from Phase 1 (above 5 absolute points in all cases). Lower casing does not seem useful for English and Swedish (0.5 improvement for English over the best result without lower casing, and no improvement for Swedish), but it gives an increase of 2 points on Spanish.

Table 3 presents the effect of adding features to represent capitalization patterns (words formed only by capital letters and words that start with a capital letter) and number types[3]. The improvements are modest for Swedish and slightly better for English (adding 0.8 points) and Spanish (almost one point).

---

[3] 'number types' differentiates numbers according to four types: only digits (1234), digits with hyphen (23-35), digits with '/' (2/2012), and measure (200_mg)).

Perceptron. Phase 5 (POS)				
Features	**Model**	**EN**	**SP**	**SW**
Window size	pos(0)	61.90	**70.01**	65.55
	pos(-1, +1)	**63.80**	69.95	65.50
	pos(-2, +2)	63.10	68.94	66.21

Table 5: Results adding features based on POS tags on the best model of the previous phase.

Perceptron. Phase 6 (Snomed CT, ...)				
Features	**Model**	**EN**	**SP**	**SW**
Window size	snomed(0)	66.20	68.22	**68.41**
	snomed(-2, +2)	**66.40**	67.84	68.27
	snomed(-2, +2)	65.60	67.67	68.31

Table 6: Results adding features based on Snomed tags.

Using lemmatization, Table 4 shows that we get an improvement on English (+0.3) and a decrease for Spanish and Swedish. This seems surprising, as in principle lemmatization could be useful to normalize terms (e.g. singular/plural and feminine/masculine in Spanish). Note that, as we are performing a greedy approach, the number of features used grows from one phase to the next one, and this is the main reason why we limited the number of feature templates, because the gains are decreasing for each phase. It should be clear that our experiments do not conclude that lemmatization is not useful but, rather, they show that it is not useful after applying other features. Table 5 shows the results using POS features, helpful for English and Spanish, but not for Swedish. We hypothesize that it could be due to the poorer quality of the Swedish POS tagger (Dalianis et al., 2015). Finally, Table 6 presents the results using specialized medical dictionaries, giving the best results for English and Swedish, but no improvement for Spanish. This aspect deserves further work, because the Spanish Snomed has similar coverage to the English version regarding concepts (around 300,000), but less terms (660,000 compared to 480,000).

4 Conclusion

Standard and well-known features together with model tuning are frequently being left aside by researchers in favor of novel approaches, as though they were low-level or insignificant mechanisms. By contrast, we have showed that these simple techniques lead us to achieve significant improvements at really low computation expenses. As an example, looking at the Semeval 2014 Shared Task, we can say from our results that a simple system using only word forms and POS would outperform more than half of the presented systems[4]. It is not our aim to imply that other systems were poorly designed, as most of them had other objectives in mind, such as experimenting new approaches but, rather, our objective is to delve into the details of the simplest approaches, that are specially interesting for implemented systems, but are often neglected in scientific papers[5]. The results for our best performing systems for Swedish and Spanish are near to those obtained by more elaborated techniques like word embeddings, although they are still far from the best performing system on the Semeval English test.

To summarize, we experimented the NER task related to the biomedical domain in three languages: Semeval task in English, and EHRs in both Swedish and Spanish. The techniques presented tend to be of much benefit, particularly for domains that lack of big amounts of data, as it is the case of biomedicine:

- It is recommendable to re-case the text and well-worthy trying different window-sizes on each language (not simply using the default parameters adopted from other languages).
- While prefixes and suffixes have a different impact on each language, it seems as though taking all prefixes and suffixes of lengths 3 and 4 is a generally recommendable configuration. These techniques can be specially useful when analyzing non-formal text, as in the Spanish medical records.
- Regarding other types of information (capitalization, numbers, lemmas and POS) we have seen that, although the features can be effective, they should be carefully tested on each language and corpus.
- Overall, we see that there are important differences on the impact of different features with respect to each language. This fact opens an interesting research area for analyzing the effect of language and corpus types on the effectiveness of each feature.

For future work we will take these results as a stronger baseline and delve into state-of-the art techniques e.g. word embeddings (Bengio et al., 2006; Mikolov et al., 2013) and recursive neural networks (Lample et al., 2016) to gain an insight on their impact on medical NER for these three languages.

---

[4]Looking at Tables 5 and 6, and taking into account that the results on the test set bumped by 2 points (Pradhan et al., 2014).

[5]We think that, in fact, this low level tuning was performed for the Semeval 2014 best performing systems, although their system description papers do not address this issue in detail.

Acknowledgements

The authors would like to thank the Nordic Center of Excellence in Health-Related e-Sciences (NIASC) and the personnel of Pharmacy and Pharmacovigilance services of the Galdakao-Usansolo Hospital and the Pharmacy service of the Basurto Hospital. This work was partially funded by the Spanish Ministry of Science and Innovation (EXTRECM: TIN2013-46616-C2-1-R, TADEEP: TIN2015-70214-P) and the Basque Government (DETEAMI: Department of Health 2014111003).

References

Rodrigo Agerri and German Rigau. 2016. Robust multilingual named entity recognition with shallow semi-supervised features. *Artificial Intelligence*, 238:63–82.

Giuseppe Attardi, Vittoria Cozza, and Daniele Sartiano. 2014. Unipi: Recognition of mentions of disorders in clinical text. In *Proceedings of the 8th International Workshop on Semantic Evaluation (SemEval 2014)*, pages 754–760, Dublin, Ireland, August. Association for Computational Linguistics and Dublin City University.

Yoshua Bengio, Holger Schwenk, Jean-Sébastien Senécal, Fréderic Morin, and Jean-Luc Gauvain. 2006. Neural probabilistic language models. In *Innovations in Machine Learning*, pages 137–186. Springer.

W. Boag, K. Wacome, T. Naumann, and A. Rumshisky. 2010. Cliner: A lightweight tool for clinical named entity recognition. *Journal of the American Medical Informatics Association*, 17(5):507–513.

Peter F Brown, Peter V Desouza, Robert L Mercer, Vincent J Della Pietra, and Jenifer C Lai. 1992. Class-based n-gram models of natural language. *Computational linguistics*, 18(4):467–479.

Alexander Clark. 2003. Combining distributional and morphological information for part of speech induction. In *Proceedings of the tenth conference on European chapter of the Association for Computational Linguistics-Volume 1*, pages 59–66. Association for Computational Linguistics.

Michael Collins. 2002. Discriminative training meth- ods for hidden markov models: Theory and ex- periments with perceptron algorithms. In *Proceedings of the 2002 Conference on Empirical Methods in Natural Language Processing*, pages 1–8. Association for Computational Linguistics, July.

Hercules Dalianis, Aron Henriksson, Maria Kvist, Sumithra Velupillai, and Rebecka Weegar. 2015. Health bank– a workbench for data science applications in healthcare. In *Proceedings of the CAiSE-2015 Industry Track co-located with 27th Conference on Advanced Information Systems Engineering (CAiSE 2015)*, volume 1381, pages 1–18. CEUR, urn:nbn:de:0074-1381-0.

Cicero dos Santos and Victor Guimarães. 2015. Boosting named entity recognition with neural character embeddings. In *Proceedings of the Fifth Named Entity Workshop*, pages 25–33, Beijing, China, July. Association for Computational Linguistics.

Yoav Freund and Robert E. Schapire. 1999. Large margin classification using the perceptron algorithm. *Machine Learning*, 37(3):277–296.

IHTSDO. 2016. SNOMED-CT, Systematized Nomenclature of Medicine-Clinical Terms, http://www.ihtsdo.org/snomed-ct/. Accessed 2014-04-09.

Rohit Kate. 2014. Uwm: Applying an existing trainable semantic parser to parse robotic spatial commands. In *Proceedings of the 8th International Workshop on Semantic Evaluation (SemEval 2014)*, pages 823–827, Dublin, Ireland, August. Association for Computational Linguistics and Dublin City University.

Taku Kudo and Yuji Matsumoto. 2001. Chunking with support vector machines. In *Proceedings of the second meeting of the North American Chapter of the Association for Computational Linguistics on Language technologies*, pages 1–8. Association for Computational Linguistics, 2001.

Taku Kudo. 2013. CRF++: yet another CRF toolkit. https://taku910.github.io/crfpp//.

Guillaume Lample, Miguel Ballesteros, Sandeep Subramanian, Kazuya Kawakami, and Chris Dyer. 2016. Neural architectures for named entity recognition. *arXiv preprint arXiv:1603.01360*.

André Leal, Diogo Gonçalves, Bruno Martins, and Francisco M Couto. 2014. Ulisboa: Identification and classification of medical concepts. In *Proceedings of the 8th International Workshop on Semantic Evaluation*, pages 711–715.

Tomas Mikolov, Ilya Sutskever, Kai Chen, Greg S Corrado, and Jeff Dean. 2013. Distributed representations of words and phrases and their compositionality. In *Advances in neural information processing systems*, pages 3111–3119.

Maite Oronoz, Arantza Casillas, Koldo Gojenola, and Alicia Perez. 2013. Automatic Annotation of Medical Records in Spanish with Disease, Drug and Substance Names. In *Lecture Notes in Computer Science, 8259. Progress in Pattern Recognition, ImageAnalysis, ComputerVision, and Applications 18th Iberoamerican Congress, CIARP 2013, Havana, Cuba*, November 20-23.

Maite Oronoz, Koldo Gojenola, Alicia Prez, Arantza Daz de Ilarraza, and Arantza Casillas. 2015. On the creation of a clinical gold standard corpus in spanish: Mining adverse drug reactions. *Journal of Biomedical Informatics*, 56:318 – 332.

Robert Östling. 2013. Stagger: An open-source part of speech tagger for Swedish. *Northern European Journal of Language Technology*, 3:1–18.

Ankur Parikh, Avinesh PVS, Joy Mustafi, Lalit Agarwalla, and Ashish Mungi. 2014. Thinkminers: Disorder recognition using conditional random fields and distributional semantics. In *Proceedings of the 8th International Workshop on Semantic Evaluation (SemEval 2014)*, pages 652–656, Dublin, Ireland, August. Association for Computational Linguistics and Dublin City University.

Sameer Pradhan, Noémie Elhadad, Wendy Chapman, Suresh Manandhar, and Guergana Savova. 2014. Semeval-2014 task 7: Analysis of clinical text. In *Proceedings of the 8th International Workshop on Semantic Evaluation (SemEval 2014)*, pages 54–62, Dublin, Ireland, August. Association for Computational Linguistics and Dublin City University.

Sv Ramanan, Chennai Adyar, and Senthil Nathan. 2014. Relagent: Entity detection and normalization for diseases in clinical records: A linguistically driven approach. *SemEval 2014*, page 477.

Lev Ratinov and Dan Roth. 2009. Design challenges and misconceptions in named entity recognition. In *Proceedings of the Thirteenth Conference on Computational Natural Language Learning*, pages 147–155. Association for Computational Linguistics.

Guergana K Savova, James J Masanz, Philip V Ogren, Jiaping Zheng, Sunghwan Sohn, Karin C Kipper-Schuler, and Christopher G Chute. 2010. Mayo clinical text analysis and knowledge extraction system (ctakes): architecture, component evaluation and applications. *Journal of the American Medical Informatics Association*, 17(5):507–513.

Joseph Turian, Lev-Arie Ratinov, and Yoshua Bengio. 2010. Word representations: A simple and general method for semi-supervised learning. In *Proceedings of the 48th Annual Meeting of the Association for Computational Linguistics*, pages 384–394, Uppsala, Sweden, July. Association for Computational Linguistics.

Bidirectional LSTM-CRF for Clinical Concept Extraction

Raghavendra Chalapathy
University of Sydney
Capital Markets CRC
rcha9612@uni.sydney.edu.au

Ehsan Zare Borzeshi
Capital Markets CRC
ezborzeshi@cmcrc.com

Massimo Piccardi
University of Technology Sydney
Massimo.Piccardi@uts.edu.au

Abstract

Automated extraction of concepts from patient clinical records is an essential facilitator of clinical research. For this reason, the 2010 i2b2/VA Natural Language Processing Challenges for Clinical Records introduced a concept extraction task aimed at identifying and classifying concepts into predefined categories (i.e., treatments, tests and problems). State-of-the-art concept extraction approaches heavily rely on handcrafted features and domain-specific resources which are hard to collect and define. For this reason, this paper proposes an alternative, streamlined approach: a recurrent neural network (the bidirectional LSTM with CRF decoding) initialized with general-purpose, off-the-shelf word embeddings. The experimental results achieved on the 2010 i2b2/VA reference corpora using the proposed framework outperform all recent methods and ranks closely to the best submission from the original 2010 i2b2/VA challenge.

1 Introduction

Patient clinical records typically contain longitudinal data about patients' health status, diseases, conducted tests and response to treatments. Analysing such information can prove of immense value not only for clinical practice, but also for the organisation and management of healthcare services. *Concept extraction* (CE) aims to identify mentions to medical concepts such as problems, test and treatments in clinical records (e.g., discharge summaries and progress reports) and classify them into predefined categories. The concepts in clinical records are often expressed with unstructured, "free" text, making their automatic extraction a challenging task for clinical Natural Language Processing (NLP) systems. Traditional approaches have extensively relied on rule-based systems and lexicons to recognise the concepts of interest. Typically, the concepts represent drug names, anatomical nomenclature and other specialized names and phrases which are not part of everyday vocabularies. For instance, "resp status" should be interpreted as "response status". Such use of abbreviated phrases and acronyms is very common within the medical community, with many abbreviations having a specific meaning that differ from that of other lexicons. Dictionary-based systems perform concept extraction by looking up terms on medical ontologies such as the Unified Medical Language System (UMLS) (Kipper-Schuler et al., 2008). Intrinsically, dictionary- and rule-based systems are laborious to implement and inflexible to new cases and misspellings (Liu et al., 2015). Although these systems can achieve high precision, they tend to suffer from low recall (i.e., they may miss a significant number of concepts). To overcome these limitations, various machine learning approaches have been proposed (e.g., conditional random fields (CRFs), maximum-entropy classifiers and support vector machines) to simultaneously exploit the textual and contextual information while reducing the reliance on lexicon lookup (Lafferty et al., 2001; Berger et al., 1996; Joachims, 1998). State-of-the-art machine learning approaches usually follow a two-step process of *feature engineering* and *classification*. The feature engineering task is, in its own right, very laborious and demanding on expert knowledge, and it can become the bottleneck of the overall approach. For this reason, this paper proposes a highly streamlined alternative: to employ a contemporary neural network - the bidirectional LSTM-CRF - initialized with general-purpose, off-the-shelf word embeddings such

Proceedings of the Clinical Natural Language Processing Workshop,
pages 7–12, Osaka, Japan, December 11-17 2016.

Sentence	His	HCT	had	dropped	from	36.7	despite	2U	PRBC	and
Concept class	O	B-test	O	O	O	O	O	B-treatment	I-treatment	O

Table 1: Example sentence in a concept extraction task. The concept classes are represented in the standard in/out/begin (IOB) format.

as GloVe (Pennington et al., 2014a) and Word2Vec (Mikolov et al., 2013b). The experimental results over the authoritative 2010 i2b2/VA benchmark show that the proposed approach outperforms all recent approaches and ranks closely to the best from the literature.

2 Related Work

Most of the research to date has framed CE as a specialized case of named-entity recognition (NER) and employed a number of supervised and semi-supervised machine learning algorithms with domain-dependent attributes and text features (Uzuner et al., 2011). Hybrid models obtained by cascading CRF and SVM classifiers along with several pattern-matching rules have shown to produce effective results (Boag et al., 2015). Moreover, (Fu and Ananiadou, 2014) have given evidence to the importance of including preprocessing steps such as truecasing and annotation combination. The system that has reported the highest accuracy on the 2010 i2b2/VA concept extraction benchmark is based on unsupervised feature representations obtained by Brown clustering and a hidden semi-Markov model as classifier (de-Bruijn et al., 2011). However, the use of a "hard" clustering technique such as Brown clustering is not suitable for capturing multiple relations between the words and the concepts. For this reason, Jonnalagadda et al. (Jonnalagadda et al., 2012) demonstrated that a random indexing model with distributed word representations can improve clinical concept extraction. Moreover, Wu et al. (Wu et al., 2015) have jointly used word embeddings derived from the entire English Wikipedia (Collobert et al., 2011) and binarized word embeddings derived from domain-specific corpora (e.g. the MIMIC-II corpus (Saeed et al., 2011)). In the broader field of machine learning, the recent years have witnessed a proliferation of deep neural networks, with outstanding results in tasks as diverse as visual, speech and named-entity recognition (Hinton et al., 2012; Krizhevsky et al., 2012; Lample et al., 2016). One of the main advantages of neural networks over traditional approaches is that they can learn the feature representations automatically from the data, thus avoiding the expensive feature-engineering stage. Given the promising performance of deep neural networks and the recent success of unsupervised word embeddings in general NLP tasks (Pennington et al., 2014a; Mikolov et al., 2013b; Lebret and Collobert, 2014), this paper sets to explore the use of a state-of-the-art deep sequential model initialized with general-purpose word embeddings for a task of clinical concept extraction.

3 The Proposed Approach

CE can be formulated as a joint segmentation and classification task over a predefined set of classes. As an example, consider the input sentence provided in Table 1. The notation follows the widely adopted in/out/begin (IOB) entity representation with, in this instance, *HCT* as the test and *2U PRBC* as the treatment. In this paper, we approach the CE task by the bidirectional LSTM-CRF framework where each word in the input sentence is first mapped to either a random vector or a vector from a word embedding. We therefore provide a brief description of both word embeddings and the model hereafter.

Word embeddings are vector representations of natural language words that aim to preserve the semantic and syntactic similarities between them. The vector representations can be generated by either count-based approaches such as Hellinger-PCA (Lebret and Collobert, 2014) or trained models such as Word2Vec (including skip-grams and continuous-bag-of-words) and GloVe trained over large, unsupervised corpora of general-nature documents. In its embedded representation, each word in a text is represented by a real-valued vector, x, of arbitrary dimensionality, d.

Recurrent neural networks (RNNs) are a family of neural networks that operate on sequential data. They take as input a sequence of vectors $(x_1, x_2, ..., x_n)$ and output a sequence of class posterior probabilities, $(y_1, y_2, ..., y_n)$. An intermediate layer of hidden nodes, $(h_1, h_2, ..., h_n)$, is also part of the model.

	Training set	Test set
notes	170	256
sentences	16315	27626
problem	7073	12592
test	4608	9225
treatment	4844	9344

Table 2: Statistics of the training and test data sets used for the 2010-i2b2/VA concept extraction.

In an RNN, the value of the hidden node at time t, h_t, depends on both the current input, x_t, and the previous hidden node, h_{t-1}. This recurrent connection from the past timeframe enables a form of short-term memory and makes the RNNs suitable for the prediction of sequences. Formally, the value of a hidden node is described as:

$$h_t = f(U \bullet x_t + V \bullet h_{t-1}) \tag{1}$$

where U and V are trained weight matrices between the input and the hidden layer, and between the past and current hidden layers, respectively. Function $f(\cdot)$ is the sigmoid function, $f(x) = 1/1 + e^{-x}$, that adds non-linearity to the layer. Eventually, $h(t)$ is input into the output layer and convolved with the output weight matrix, W:

$$y_t = g(W \bullet h_t), \text{ with } g(z_m) = \frac{e^{z_m}}{\Sigma_{k=1}^{K} e^{z_k}} \tag{2}$$

Eventually, the output is normalized by a multi-class logistic function, $g(\cdot)$, to become a proper probability over the class set. Therefore, the output dimensionality is equal to the number of concept classes. Although an RNN can, in theory, learn long-term dependencies, in practice it tends to be biased towards its most recent inputs. For this reason, the Long Short-Term Memory (LSTM) network incorporates an additional "gated" memory cell that can store long-range dependencies (Hochreiter and Schmidhuber, 1997). In its bidirectional version, the LSTM computes both a forward, $\overrightarrow{h_t}$, and a backward, $\overleftarrow{h_t}$, hidden representation at each timeframe t. The final representation is created by concatenating them as $h_t = [\overrightarrow{h_t}; \overleftarrow{h_t}]$. In all these networks, the hidden layer can be regarded as an implicit, learned feature that enables concept prediction. A further improvement to this model is provided by performing joint decoding of the entire input sequence in a Viterbi-style manner using a CRF (Lafferty et al., 2001) as the final output layer. The resulting network is commonly referred to as the *bidirectional LSTM-CRF* (Lample et al., 2016).

4 Experiments

4.1 Dataset

The 2010 i2b2/VA Natural Language Processing Challenges for Clinical Records include a concept extraction task focused on the extraction of medical concepts from patient reports. For the challenge, a total of 394 concept-annotated reports for training, 477 for testing, and 877 unannotated reports were de-identified and released to the participants alongside a data use agreement (Uzuner et al., 2011). However, part of this data set is no longer being distributed due to restrictions later introduced by the Institutional Review Board (IRB). Thus, Table 2 summarizes the basic statistics of the training and test data sets which are currently publicly available and that we have used in our experiments.

4.2 Evaluation Methodology

Our models have been blindly evaluated on the 2010 i2b2/VA CE test data using a strict evaluation criterion requiring the predicted concepts to exactly match the annotated concepts in terms of both boundary

Methods	Precision	Recall	F$_1$ Score
Hidden semi-Markov Model (deBruijn et al., 2011)	86.88	83.64	85.23
Distributonal Semantics CRF (Jonnalagadda et al., 2012)	85.60	82.00	83.70
Binarized Neural Embedding CRF (Wu et al., 2015)	85.10	80.60	82.80
CliNER (Boag et al., 2015)	79.50	81.20	80.00
Truecasing CRFSuite (Fu and Ananiadou, 2014)	80.83	71.47	75.86
Random - Bidirectional LSTM-CRF	81.06	75.40	78.13
Word2Vec - Bidirectional LSTM-CRF	82.61	80.03	81.30
GloVe - Bidirectional LSTM-CRF	84.36	83.41	83.88

Table 3: Performance comparison between the bidirectional LSTM-CRF (bottom three lines) and state-of-the-art systems (top five lines) over the 2010 i2b2/VA concept extraction task.

and class. To facilitate the replication of our experimental results, we have used a publicly-available library for the implementation of the LSTM (i.e. the Theano neural network toolkit (Bergstra et al., 2010)) and we publicly release our code[1]. We have split the training set into two parts (sized at approximately 70% and 30%, respectively), using the first for training and the second for selection of the hyper-parameters ("validation") (Bergstra and Bengio, 2012).The hyper-parameters include the embedding dimension, d, chosen over $\{50, 100, 300, 500\}$, and two additional parameters, the learning and drop-out rates, that were sampled from a uniform distribution in the range $[0.05, 0.1]$. All weight matrices were randomly initialized from the uniform distribution within range $[-1, 1]$. The word embeddings were either initialized randomly in the same way or fetched from Word2Vec and GloVe (Mikolov et al., 2013a; Pennington et al., 2014b). Approximately 25% of the tokens were alphanumeric, abbreviated or domain-specific strings that were not available as pre-trained embeddings and were always randomly initialized. Early stopping of training was set to 50 epochs to mollify over-fitting, and the model that gave the best performance on the validation set was retained. The accuracy is reported in terms of micro-average F$_1$ score computed using the CoNLL score function (Nadeau and Sekine, 2007).

4.3 Results and Analysis

Table 3 shows the performance comparison between state-of-the-art CE systems and the proposed bidirectional LSTM-CRF with different initialization strategies. As a first note, the bidirectional LSTM-CRF initialized with GloVe outperforms all recent approaches (2012-2015). On the other hand, the best submission from the 2010 i2b2/VA challenge (deBruijn et al., 2011) still outperforms our approach. However, based on the description provided in (Uzuner et al., 2011), these results are not directly comparable since the experiments in (deBruijn et al., 2011; Jonnalagadda et al., 2012) had used the original dataset which has a significantly larger number of training samples. Using general-purpose, pre-trained embeddings improves the F$_1$ score by over 5 percentage points over a random initialization. In general, the results achieved with the proposed approach are close and in many cases above the results achieved by systems based on hand-engineered features.

Conclusion

This paper has explored the effectiveness of the contemporary bidirectional LSTM-CRF for clinical concept extraction. The most appealing feature of this approach is its ability to provide end-to-end recognition using general-purpose, off-the-shelf word embeddings, thus sparing effort from time-consuming feature construction. The experimental results over the authoritative 2010 i2b2/VA reference corpora look promising, with the bidirectional LSTM-CRF outperforming all recent approaches and ranking closely to the best submission from the original 2010 i2b2/VA challenge. A potential way to further improve its performance would be to explore the use of unsupervised word embeddings trained from domain-specific resources such as the MIMIC-III corpora (Johnson et al., 2016).

---

[1]https://github.com/raghavchalapathy/Bidirectional-LSTM-CRF-for-Clinical-Concept-Extraction

References

Adam L Berger, Vincent J Della Pietra, and Stephen A Della Pietra. 1996. A maximum entropy approach to natural language processing. *Computational linguistics*, 22(1):39–71.

James Bergstra and Yoshua Bengio. 2012. Random search for hyper-parameter optimization. *Journal of Machine Learning Research (JMLR)*, 13:281–305.

James Bergstra, Olivier Breuleux, Frédéric Bastien, Pascal Lamblin, Razvan Pascanu, Guillaume Desjardins, Joseph Turian, David Warde-Farley, and Yoshua Bengio. 2010. Theano: A CPU and GPU math compiler in Python. In *The 9th Python in Science Conference*, pages 1–7.

William Boag, Kevin Wacome, Tristan Naumann, and Anna Rumshisky. 2015. CliNER: A lightweight tool for clinical named entity recognition. In *AMIA Joint Summits on Clinical Research Informatics (poster)*.

Ronan Collobert, Jason Weston, Léon Bottou, Michael Karlen, Koray Kavukcuoglu, and Pavel Kuksa. 2011. Natural language processing (almost) from scratch. *Journal of Machine Learning Research (JMLR)*, 12:2493–2537.

Berry deBruijn, Colin Cherry, Svetlana Kiritchenko, Joel Martin, and Xiaodan Zhu. 2011. Machine-learned solutions for three stages of clinical information extraction: the state of the art at i2b2 2010. *Journal of the American Medical Informatics Association*, 18(5):557–562.

Xiao Fu and Sophia Ananiadou. 2014. Improving the extraction of clinical concepts from clinical records. *Proceedings of the 4th Workshop on Building and Evaluating Resources for Health and Biomedical Text Processing (BioTxtM04)*.

Geoffrey Hinton, Li Deng, Dong Yu, George E Dahl, Abdel-rahman Mohamed, Navdeep Jaitly, Andrew Senior, Vincent Vanhoucke, Patrick Nguyen, Tara N Sainath, et al. 2012. Deep neural networks for acoustic modeling in speech recognition: The shared views of four research groups. *IEEE Signal Processing Magazine*, 29(6):82–97.

Sepp Hochreiter and Jürgen Schmidhuber. 1997. Long short-term memory. *Neural Computation*, 9(8):1735–1780.

Thorsten Joachims. 1998. Text categorization with support vector machines: Learning with many relevant features. In *European conference on machine learning (ECML)*, pages 137–142. Springer.

Alistair E.W. Johnson, Tom J. Pollard, Lu Shen, Li-wei H. Lehman, Mengling Feng, Mohammad Ghassemi, Benjamin Moody, Peter Szolovits, Leo A. Celi, and Roger G. Mark. 2016. MIMIC-III, a freely accessible critical care database. *Scientific Data*, 3.

Siddhartha Jonnalagadda, Trevor Cohen, Stephen Wu, and Graciela Gonzalez. 2012. Enhancing clinical concept extraction with distributional semantics. *Journal of biomedical informatics*, 45(1):129–140.

Karin Kipper-Schuler, Vinod Kaggal, James Masanz, Philip Ogren, and Guergana Savova. 2008. System evaluation on a named entity corpus from clinical notes. In *Language Resources and Evaluation Conference (LREC)*, pages 3001–3007.

Alex Krizhevsky, Ilya Sutskever, and Geoffrey E Hinton. 2012. Imagenet classification with deep convolutional neural networks. In *Neural Information Processing Systems (NIPS)*.

John Lafferty, Andrew McCallum, and Fernando Pereira. 2001. Conditional random fields: Probabilistic models for segmenting and labeling sequence data. In *International Machine Learning Conference (ICML)*, pages 282–289.

Guillaume Lample, Miguel Ballesteros, Sandeep Subramanian, Kazuya Kawakami, and Chris Dyer. 2016. Neural architectures for named entity recognition. In *The North American Chapter of the Association for Computational Linguistics: Human Language Technologies (NAACL-HLT)*.

Rémi Lebret and Ronan Collobert. 2014. Word emdeddings through hellinger PCA. In *European Chapter of the Association for Computational Linguistics (EACL)*.

Shengyu Liu, Buzhou Tang, Qingcai Chen, and Xiaolong Wang. 2015. Drug name recognition: Approaches and resources. *Information*, 6(4):790–810.

Tomas Mikolov, Ilya Sutskever, Kai Chen, Greg Corrado, and Jeffrey Dean. 2013a. GloVe: Global Vectors for Word Representation. https://code.google.com/archive/p/word2vec/. Accessed: 2016-08-30.

Tomas Mikolov, Ilya Sutskever, Kai Chen, Greg S Corrado, and Jeff Dean. 2013b. Distributed representations of words and phrases and their compositionality. In *Neural Information Processing Systems (NIPS)*, pages 3111–3119.

David Nadeau and Satoshi Sekine. 2007. A survey of named entity recognition and classification. *Linguisticae Investigationes*, 30(1):3–26.

Jeffrey Pennington, Richard Socher, and Christopher D. Manning. 2014a. GloVe: Global vectors for word representation. In *European conference on machine learning (ECML)*, pages 1532–1543.

Jeffrey Pennington, Richard Socher, and Christopher D. Manning. 2014b. GloVe: Global vectors for word representation. http://nlp.stanford.edu/projects/glove/. Accessed: 2016-08-30.

Mohammed Saeed, Mauricio Villarroel, Andrew T. Reisner, Gari Clifford, Li-Wei Lehman, George Moody, Thomas Heldt, Tin H. Kyaw, Benjamin Moody, and Roger G. Mark. 2011. Multiparameter Intelligent Monitoring in Intensive Care II (MIMIC-II): A public-access intensive care unit database. *Critical Care Medicine*, 39:952–960.

Özlem Uzuner, Brett R South, Shuying Shen, and Scott L DuVall. 2011. 2010 i2b2/VA challenge on concepts, assertions, and relations in clinical text. *Journal of the American Medical Informatics Association*, 18(5):552–556.

Yonghui Wu, Jun Xu, Min Jiang, Yaoyun Zhang, and Hua Xu. 2015. A study of neural word embeddings for named entity recognition in clinical text. In *AMIA Annual Symposium Proceedings*, volume 2015.

MedNLPDoc: Japanese Shared Task for Clinical NLP

Eiji Aramaki
NAIST
aramaki@is.naist.jp

Yoshinobu Kano
Shizuoka University
kano@inf.shizuoka.ac.jp

Tomoko Ohkuma
NAIST
tomokoohkuma@gmail.com

Mizuki Morita
Okayama University
mizuki@okayama-u.ac.jp

Abstract

Due to the recent replacements of physical documents with electronic medical records (EMR), the importance of information processing in medical fields has been increased. We have been organizing the MedNLP task series in NTCIR-10 and 11. These workshops were the first shared tasks which attempt to evaluate technologies that retrieve important information from medical reports written in Japanese. In this report, we describe the NTCIR-12 MedNLPDoc task which is designed for more advanced and practical use for the medical fields. This task is considered as a multi-labeling task to a patient record. This report presents results of the shared task, discusses and illustrates remained issues in the medical natural language processing field.

1   Introduction

Medical reports using electronic media are now replacing those of paper media. Correspondingly, the information processing techniques in medical fields have radically increased their importance. Nevertheless, the information and communication technologies (ICT) in medical fields tend to be underdeveloped compared to the other fields [1].

Processing large amounts of medical reports and obtaining knowledge from them may assist precise and timely treatments. Our goal is to promote developing practical tools that support medical decisions. In order to achieve this goal, we have been organizing 'shared tasks (contests, competitions, challenge evaluations, critical assessments)' to encourage research in medical information retrieval. Among the various shared tasks, one of the best-known medical-related shared tasks is the Informatics for Integrating Biology and the Bedside (i2b2) by the National Institutes of Health (NIH), which started in 2006 [2]. The Text Retrieval Conference (TREC), which addresses more diverse issues, also launched the Medical Reports Track [3]. Shortly after the NTCIR-10 MedNLP task, the first European medical shared task, the ShARe/CLEF eHealth Evaluation Lab [4], was organized. This shared task focuses on natural language processing (NLP) and information retrieval (IR) for clinical care. While they are targeted only at English texts, medical reports are written in native languages in most countries. Therefore, information retrieval techniques in individual language are required to be developed.

We organized the NTCIR-10 and NTCIR-11 MedNLP tasks (shortly MedNLP) [5] which were the first and second shared tasks, evaluating technologies that retrieve important information from medical reports written in Japanese. These previous tasks include three sub tasks: named entity removal task (de-identification task), disease name extraction task (complaint and diagnosis), and normalization task (ICD coding task). These tasks correspond to elemental technologies for computational systems which support diverse medical services.

Following the success of these MedNLP tasks, we designed the NTCIR-12 MedNLPDoc task to be more advanced and practical. In this MedNLPDoc task, we provided a new challenging task where participants' systems infer disease names in ICD (International Codes for Diseases) from textual medical

Proceedings of the Clinical Natural Language Processing Workshop,
pages 13–16, Osaka, Japan, December 11-17 2016.

records. Due to this practical setting, task participants' systems could directly support an actual daily clinical services and clinical studies in various areas.

2   Task & Corpus

2.1   ICD Code

The International Classification of Diseases (ICD) is the standard diagnostic coding system used in many countries for epidemiology, health management and clinical purposes. It is used to monitor the incidence and prevalence of diseases and other health problems, proving a picture of the general health situation of countries and populations. In the latest version of the ICD coding system, ICD-10, each ICD code consists of a single alphabet prefix and two digits of numbers. In addition to these three characters that represents a major classification, more detailed classification can be represented by several digits of additional numbers as suffix, up to six characters in total. Because the major categories are limited to 21 sections, the major categories include a set of similar diseases.

2.2   ICD Coding Task

We provided a training data set of medical records that is taken from "ICD Coding Training, Second Edition", written in Japanese for training Health Information Managers (HIMs). We organized the phenotyping task, in which the participants are required to assign ICD-10 code(s) to a given medical record.

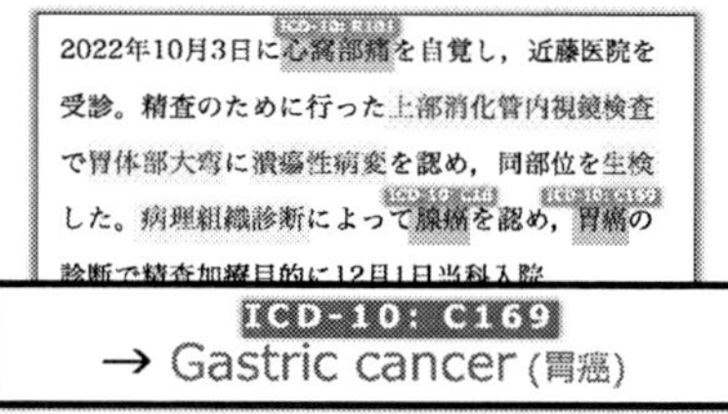

Figure 1: coding task: The participants will assign ICD-10 codes from texts. This example should be assigned as C169, which means Gastric cancer. In this case, only one ICD-10 code was assigned, but in general, one or more codes should be assigned.

Table 1: Number of Code Assigned.

	# (valiance)	Min.	Max.
SURE	2.8 ($\pm$1.6)	0	8
MAJOR	5.2 ($\pm$2.0)	1	11
POSSIBLE	9.4 ($\pm$3.8)	2	19

2.3   Corpus

We created a medical record corpus for this task which includes 278 individual medical records (200 were used for training, and the other 78 used for test). The average number of sentences per record is 7.82. The average number of codes per record is 3.86 (total 1073 codes and 552 variants). In test set, three professional human coders (more than one-year experience) individually added ICD-10 codes. We defined three different code sets as follows.

- **SURE (S):** sure code set consists of codes that all coders (three persons) utilized.
- **MAJOR (M):** major code set consists of codes that two or three coders utilized.
- **POSSIBLE (P):** possible code set consists of codes that at least one coder utilized.

We derived three types of gold standard data for each code set above. Note that there is a relationship of $S \in M \in P$ (SURE is a subset of MAJOR, MAJOR is a subset of POSSIBLE). The inter annotation ratio (**IAA**) between three humans (Human-A, Human-B, and Human-C) is defined by the following formula:

$$\textbf{IAA} = \Sigma_{d \in D} |A_d \cap B_d \cap C_d| \setminus |A_d \cup B_d \cup C_d| / |D|.$$

where D is the set of all records. $|D|$ is the number of records. $|A_d \cap B_d \cap C_d|$ is the number of SURE codes in the record d. $|A_d \cup B_d \cup C_d|$ is the number of POSSIBLE codes in the record d.

2.4   Evaluation

Performance of the coding task was assessed using the F-score (β=1), precision, and recall. Precision is the percentage of correct codes found by a participant's system. Recall is the percentage of codes presented in the corpus that were found by the system. F-score is the harmonic mean of precision and recall.

The three human coders were also evaluated by this measure. The average results are as follows: Av. Sure Precision=0.168, Av. Sure Recall=0.388, and Av. Sure F-measure=0.235.

3   Result

The participating systems are shown in Table 2. Roughly, the systems are classified into three types: (1) machine learning approach (team A, B, E, and G), (2) rule based approach (team C. D and H), and (3) their combination (team C).

3.1   Machine Learning V.S. Rule-based

The performance is shown in Figure 2. Among all systems, the highest performance system is provided by the SYSTEM-C in the SURE metrics. The system is based on heuristic rules, indicating that rule-based approaches still have its advantage. Considering machine learning approaches have been outperforming rule based approaches in most of the other NLP fields, this result is remarkable for future system designing in the medical domain.

In the other metrics (MAJOR and POSSIBLE), the system-G3 and the system E achieved better performance than the SYSTEM-C. Not like the SYSTEM-C, the SYSTEM-G3 fully implemented by the multiple machine learning methods. Also, the SYSTEM E system partly utilized machine learning, but it also employs rule-based features that represent coding heuristics.

In summary, the overall result indicates the advantages of traditional rule based approach. These results were caused by two reasons: (1) the corpus size of this task is relatively small than the other tasks, and (2) the classification space (the number of code) is huge. This result revealed that current machine learning techniques still suffer from such conditions.

3.2   Contribution of Extra Resources

Another viewpoint of this task is the contribution of extra resources. Almost all participants used the MEDIS Standard Masters (MDS) and some used other language resources. While this implies that a medical dictionary is the most useful tool to this task. The SYSTEM-D calculated similarity scores between medical vocabulary n-grams and word n-grams in EMR. The SYSTEM-H calculated edit-distances and used their scores as features of CRF. The SYSTEM-A used three dictionaries in addition to MDS. They used *Kuromoji* morphological analyzer with their customized dictionary. In summary, most of the teams have relied on the existing language resources, and its quality and quantity varies the team performance.

3.3   Strategy

The strategies of the systems are characterized by two parameters; (1) the average number of codes and (2) the variance of codes. Table 3 presents the average number of codes assigned by the high performance three systems (SYSTEM C, E, and G3). The SYSTEM-G3 assigns more codes rather than the others (high recall-oriented). In contrast, the SYSTEM-C ascend only 2.0 codes in average (high precision-oriented).

Another parameter is the distribution of codes. Figure 3 shows the distribution of codes of these systems. The SYSTEM-C handles a narrow coding spaces, in which the most of codes are assigned in Z**, R** or C**. This also indicates that the SYSTEM-C aims to obtain the high precision.

Table 2: participant system.

Team	Sources	Methods
A	ICD-10(en), Wikipedia, Google/Yandex MT, HUG(fr)	rule base
B	MDS, ICD-10	machine learning (CRF)/ Edit distance (as features)
C	MDS, Wikipedia	Rule based
D	MDS, ICD training book	string similarity measure
E	MDS	Rule based (as features), machine learning (CRF)
F	MDS, training data	search engine (using named entity based keywords?)
G	MDS	machine learning (CRF,LIBLINER (SVM))
H	MDS	NA (Exact Match)

* MDS indicates the ICD Dictionary, MEDIS Standard Masters.

* CRF indicates the conditional random fields.

Table 3: Number of Code Assigned.

SYSTEM	# of codes	Min.	Max.
C	2.0	0	7
E	3.4	1	8
G3	6.6	8	14

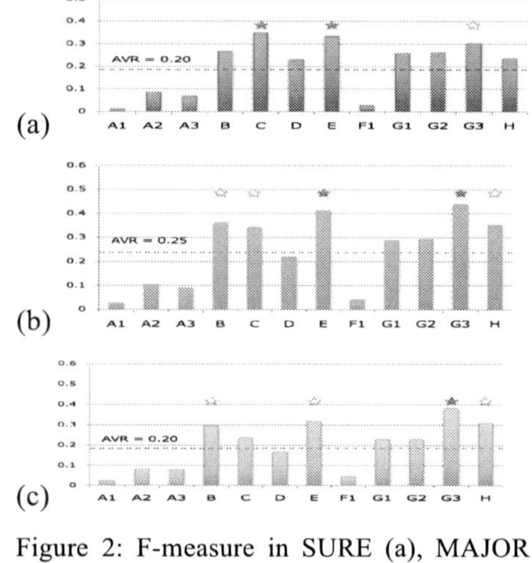

Figure 2: F-measure in SURE (a), MAJOR (b), and POSSIBLE (c).

	C	E	G3	SURE	MAJOR	POSS.
A00-B99	1	4	9	1	3	7
C00-D48	20	16	15	8	10	16
D50-D89	0	0	21	0	1	15
E00-E90	1	22	25	7	18	39
F00-F99	1	0	1	1	2	6
G00-G99	2	1	4	1	3	11
H00-H59	0	1	1	0	1	3
H60-H95	0	2	5	0	1	4
I00-I99	5	29	36	32	39	63
J00-J99	1	11	22	6	13	32
K00-K93	2	18	21	4	9	20
L00-L99	1	2	44	1	4	8
M00-M99	0	3	1	0	0	6
N00-N99	0	5	7	4	4	10
O00-O99	0	0	0	0	0	0
P00-P96	0	0	0	0	0	0
Q00-Q99	0	0	2	0	0	0
R00-R99	41	135	288	73	183	358
S00-T98	19	14	22	3	14	35
V01-Y98	0	0	0	2	4	15
Z00-Z99	77	0	6	75	92	147
U00-U99	0	0	0	0	0	0

Figure 3: Code Distribution of the best three systems.

4   Conclusion

This paper describes the NTCIR-12 MedNLPDoc task which is a multi-labeling task, ICD-10 coding, to a patient record. This report presents results of the shared task, discusses and illustrates remained issues in the medical natural language processing field. Still, rule-based approaches have demonstrated the advantage in this task, requiring the future development of machine learning approaches that deal with small data.

Reference

[1] [r Chapman, W.W., Nadkarni, P.M., Hirschman, L., D'Avolio, L.W., Savova, G.K., and Uzuner, O. 2011. Overcoming barriers to NLP for clinical text: the role of shared tasks and the need for additional creative solutions. *J Am Med Inform Assoc*, 18, 540–543.

[2] Ozlem, U. 2008. Second i2b2 workshop on natural language processing challenges for clinical records, in *AMIA Annual Symposium proceedings*. 1252-1253.

[3] Voorhees, E.M. and Hersh, W. 2012. Overview of the TREC 2012 Medical Records Track. in The Twentieth Text REtrieval Conference.

[4] ShARe/CLEF eHealth Evaluation Lab. 2013 [cited 2014/06/04; Available from: https://sites.google.com/site/shareclefe-health/].

[5] Morita, M., Kano, Y., Ohkuma, T., Miyabe M., and Aramaki, E. 2013. Overview of the NTCIR-10 MedNLP task, In *Proceedings of NTCIR-10*.

Feature-Augmented Neural Networks for Patient Note De-identification

Ji Young Lee[1]*, Franck Dernoncourt[1]*, Özlem Uzuner[2], Peter Szolovits[1]
[1]MIT, [2]SUNY Albany

{jjylee,francky}@mit.edu, ouzuner@albany.edu, psz@mit.edu

* These authors contributed equally to this work.

Abstract

Patient notes contain a wealth of information of potentially great interest to medical investigators. However, to protect patients' privacy, Protected Health Information (PHI) must be removed from the patient notes before they can be legally released, a process known as patient note de-identification. The main objective for a de-identification system is to have the highest possible recall. Recently, the first neural-network-based de-identification system has been proposed, yielding state-of-the-art results. Unlike other systems, it does not rely on human-engineered features, which allows it to be quickly deployed, but does not leverage knowledge from human experts or from electronic health records (EHRs). In this work, we explore a method to incorporate human-engineered features as well as features derived from EHRs to a neural-network-based de-identification system. Our results show that the addition of features, especially the EHR-derived features, further improves the state-of-the-art in patient note de-identification, including for some of the most sensitive PHI types such as patient names. Since in a real-life setting patient notes typically come with EHRs, we recommend developers of de-identification systems to leverage the information EHRs contain.

1 Introduction and related work

Medical practitioners increasingly store patient data in Electronic Health Records (EHRs) (Hsiao et al., 2011), which represents a considerable opportunity for medical investigators to construct novel models and experiments to improve patient care. Some governments even subsidize the adoption of EHRs, such as the Centers for Medicare & Medicaid Services in the United States who have spent over \$30 billion in EHR incentive payments to hospitals and medical providers (McCann, 2015).

A legal prerequisite for a patient note to be shared with a medical investigator is that it must be de-identified. The objective of the de-identification process is to remove all Protected Health Information (PHI). Not appropriately removing PHI may result in financial penalties (DesRoches et al., 2013; Wright et al., 2013). In the United States, the Health Insurance Portability and Accountability Act (HIPAA) (Office for Civil Rights, 2002) defines PHI types that must be removed, ranging from phone numbers to patient names. Failure to accurately de-identify a patient note would jeopardize the patient's privacy: the performance of a de-identification system is therefore critical.

A naive approach to de-identification is to manually identify PHI. However, this is costly (Douglass et al., 2005; Douglas et al., 2004) and unreliable (Neamatullah et al., 2008). Consequently, there has been much work developing automated de-identification systems. These systems are either based on rules or machine-learning models. Rule-based systems typically rely on patterns, expressed as regular expressions and gazetteers, defined and tuned by humans (Berman, 2003; Beckwith et al., 2006; Fielstein et al., 2004; Friedlin and McDonald, 2008; Gupta et al., 2004; Morrison et al., 2009; Neamatullah et al., 2008; Ruch et al., 2000; Sweeney, 1996; Thomas et al., 2002).

Machine-learning-based systems train a classifier to label each token as PHI or not PHI. Some systems are more fine-grained by detecting which PHI type a token belongs to. Different statistical methods have been explored for patient note de-identification, including decision trees (Szarvas et al., 2006), log-linear models, support vector machines (SVMs) (Guo et al., 2006; Uzuner et al., 2008; Hara, 2006), and conditional random field (CRFs) (Aberdeen et al., 2010). A thorough review of existing systems can be found in (Meystre et al., 2010; Stubbs et al., 2015).

Proceedings of the Clinical Natural Language Processing Workshop,
pages 17–22, Osaka, Japan, December 11-17 2016.

A more recent system has introduced the use of artificial neural networks (ANNs) for de-identification (Dernoncourt et al., 2016), and obtained state-of-the-art results. The system does not use any manually-curated features. Instead, it solely relies on character and token embeddings. While this allows the system to be developed and deployed faster, it fails to give users the possibility to add features engineered by human experts. Additionally, in practical settings of de-identification, patient notes typically come from a hospital EHR database, which contains metadata such as which patient each note pertains to, and other information such as the names of all doctors who work at the hospital where the patient was treated. The features derived from EHR databases may be useful for boosting the performance of de-identification systems. In this work, we present a method to incorporate features to this ANN-based system, and show that it further improves the state-of-the-art.

2 Method

The first model based on ANNs for patient note de-identification was introduced in (Dernoncourt et al., 2016): we extend upon their model. They utilized both token and character embeddings to learn effective features from data by fine-tuning the parameters. The main components of the ANN model are Long Short Term Memories (LSTMs) (Hochreiter and Schmidhuber, 1997), which are a type of recurrent neural networks (RNNs).

The model is composed of three layers: a character-enhanced token embedding layer, a label prediction layer, and a label sequence optimization layer. The character-enhanced token embedding layer maps each token into a vector representation. The sequence of vector representations corresponding to a sequence of tokens are input to the label prediction layer, which outputs the sequence of vectors containing the probability of each label for each corresponding token. Lastly, the sequence optimization layer outputs the most likely sequence of predicted labels based on the sequence of probability vectors from the previous layer. All layers are learned jointly. For more details on the basic ANN model, see (Dernoncourt et al., 2016).

We augment this ANN model by adding features that are human-engineered or derived from EHR database, as presented in Table 1. The majority of human-engineered features are taken from (Filannino and Nenadic, 2015), a few more features come from (Yang and Garibaldi, 2015), and additional gazetteers are collected using online resources. All features are binary and computed for each token. The binary feature vector comprising all features for a given token is fed into a feedforward neural network, the output vector of which is concatenated to the corresponding token embeddings, at the output of the character-enhanced token embedding layer, as Figure 1 illustrates.

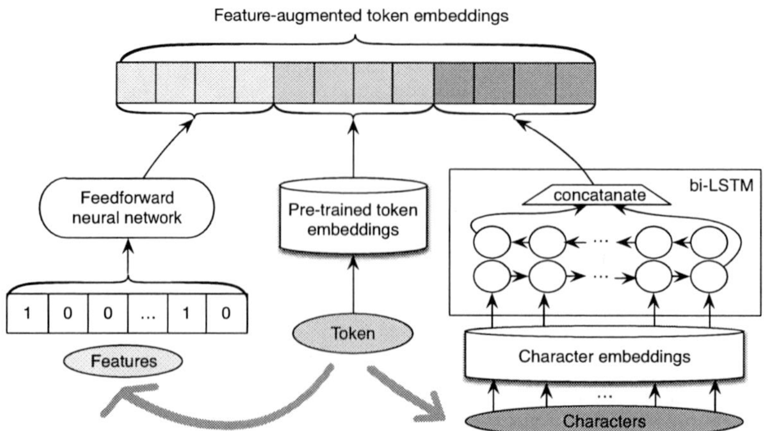

Figure 1: Feature-augmented token embeddings. Each token is mapped to a token embedding that is the concatenation of three elements: the output of a feedforward neural network that takes the features as input, a pre-trained token embedding, and the output of a bidirectional-LSTM (bi-LSTM) that takes the character embeddings as input.

Feature types	Features	
Note metadata	Patient's first name, patient's last name	EHR features
Hospital data	Doctor's first names, doctor's last names	
Morphological	Ends with s, is the first letter capitalized, contains a digit, is numeric, is alphabetic, is alphanumeric, is title case, is all lower case, is all upper case, is a stop word	
Semantic/Wordnet	Hypernyms, senses, lemma names	
Temporal	Seasons, months, weekdays, times of the day, years, years followed by apostrophe, festivity dates, holidays, cardinal numbers, decades, fuzzy quantifier (e.g., "approximately", "few"), future trigger (e.g., "next", "tomorrow")	
Gazetteers	Honorifics for doctors, honorifics, medical specialists, medical specialties, first names, last names, last name prefixes, street suffixes, US cities, US states (including abbreviations), countries, nationalities, organizations, professions	
Regular expressions	Email, age, date, phone, zip code, id number, medical record number	

Table 1: Feature list. Note metadata and hospital data are derived from the EHR database. Morphological, semantic/wordnet, and temporal features are commonly used features for NLP tasks. Gazetteers and regular expressions are specifically engineered for the task.

3 Experiments

We evaluate our model on the de-identification dataset introduced in (Dernoncourt et al., 2016), which is a subset of the MIMIC-III dataset (Goldberger et al., 2000; Saeed et al., 2011; Johnson et al., 2016), using the same train/validation/test split (70%/10%/20%). We chose this dataset as each note comes with metadata, such as the patient's name, and it is the largest de-identification dataset available to us. It contains 1,635 discharge summaries, 2,945,228 tokens, 69,525 unique tokens, and 78,633 PHI tokens.

The model is trained using stochastic gradient descent, updating all parameters, i.e., token embeddings, character embeddings, parameters of bidirectional LSTMs, and transition probabilities, at each gradient step. For regularization, dropout is applied to the character-enhanced token embeddings before the label prediction layer. We set the character embedding dimension to 25, the character-based token embedding LSTM dimension to 25, the token embedding dimension to 100, the label prediction LSTM dimension to 100, the dropout probability to 0.5, and we use GloVe embeddings (Pennington et al., 2014) trained on Wikipedia and Gigaword 5 (Parker et al., 2011) articles as pre-trained token embeddings. The hyperparameters were optimized based on the performance on the validation set.

4 Results

Table 2 presents the main results. The epochs for which the results are reported are optimized based on either the highest F1-score or the highest recall on the validation set. As expected, choosing the epoch based on the recall improves the recall on the test set, while lowering the precision. Overall, adding features consistently improves the results.

Table 3 details the results for each PHI type. The system using only the EHR features yields the highest recall for 6 out of 12 PHI types. Most importantly, the recall for patient and doctor names are higher when using features than when using no feature: this is expected as the patient name of the note and the doctor names are used as features. In fact, the two remaining false negatives for patient names are annotation errors. For example, in the sentence "The patient responded well to *Natrecor* in the past, but the improvement disappeared soon", the drug name *Natrecor* was incorrectly marked as a patient name by the human annotator. This result is highly remarkable as patient names are the most sensitive information in a patient note (South et al., 2014).

Adding all features often lowers the recall compared to using EHR features only, although the F1-score remains virtually unchanged. This is somewhat surprising, as we had expected that the features would help, as using the same feature set with a CRF to perform de-identification yields state-of-the-art results next to the ANN models (Dernoncourt et al., 2016). This could be explained as follows. Human-engineered features tend to have higher precision than recall, as it is often hard to design regular expressions or gazetteers that can detect all possible instances or variations of the desired entities. We

	Binary HIPAA (optimized by F1-score)			Binary HIPAA (optimized by recall)		
	Precision	Recall	F1-score	Precision	Recall	F1-score
No feature	99.103	99.197	99.150	98.557	99.376	98.965
EHR features	99.100	99.304	99.202	98.771	**99.441**	99.105
All features	**99.213**	**99.306**	**99.259**	**98.880**	99.420	**99.149**

Table 2: Binary HIPAA token-based results (%) for the ANN model, averaged over 5 runs. The metric refers to the detection of PHI tokens versus non-PHI tokens, amongst PHI types that are defined by HIPAA. "No feature" is the model utilizing only character and word embeddings, without any feature. "EHR features" uses only 4 features derived from EHR database: patient first name, patient last name, doctor first name, and doctor last name. "All features" makes use of all features, including the EHR features as well as other engineered features listed in Table 1. "Optimized by F1-score" and "optimized by recall" means that the epochs for which the results are reported are optimized based on the highest F1-score or the highest recall on the validation set, respectively.

	No feature			EHR features			All features			
	P	R	F1	P	R	F1	P	R	F1	Support
Zip	100.0	100.0	100.0	100.0	100.0	100.0	100.0	100.0	100.0	24
Date	98.90	99.77	99.33	98.95	**99.79**	**99.36**	**98.99**	99.69	99.34	20627
Phone	98.31	**99.58**	98.94	**98.98**	99.46	99.22	99.42	99.32	**99.37**	1438
Patient	96.89	98.34	97.61	98.62	99.14	98.88	**99.21**	**99.27**	**99.24**	302
ID	99.57	98.24	98.90	99.31	**98.82**	**99.07**	**99.77**	97.97	98.86	612
Doctor[1]	97.47	98.17	97.82	97.27	**98.48**	97.87	**97.56**	98.20	**97.88**	3676
Location	96.02	95.71	95.86	96.41	**96.49**	96.45	**96.65**	96.32	**96.46**	462
Age ≥ 90	75.12	94.29	83.60	77.04	**95.72**	**85.35**	**78.93**	93.57	84.80	28
Hospital[1]	94.78	95.39	95.08	94.77	**95.52**	95.14	**95.53**	95.50	**95.51**	1259
State[1]	99.36	**94.33**	**96.76**	**99.68**	94.03	96.73	99.39	91.94	95.49	67
Street	96.77	85.25	90.54	**97.63**	85.25	**90.96**	93.91	**86.56**	89.81	61
Country[1]	87.51	85.00	86.11	**89.29**	82.50	85.67	86.87	**95.00**	90.56	16
Binary	98.41	99.19	98.80	98.48	**99.27**	98.87	**98.61**	99.15	**98.88**	28572

Table 3: Binary token-based results (%). The reported results are optimized by recall, and averaged over 5 runs. The symbol [1] indicates that the PHI type is not required by HIPAA. The PHI type "location" designates any location that is not a street name, zip code, state or country. P stands for precision, R for recall, and F1 for F1-score.

conjecture that as the ANN model learn to rely more on such features, it might lose the ability to learn to pick up tokens that deviate from engineered features, resulting in a lower recall. For example, we notice that the phone PHI tokens that are not detected by the model using all features but are detected by the other two models, are ill-formed phone numbers such as "617-554-|2395", or phone extensions such as "617-690-4031 ext 6599". Since the phone regular expressions do not capture these two examples, they are more likely to be false negatives in the model that uses the phone regular expression features.

5 Conclusion

In this paper we presented an extension of the ANN-based model for patient note de-identification that can incorporate features. We showed that adding features results in an increase of the recall, in particular features leveraging information from the associated EHRs, namely patient names and doctor names. Our results suggest that constructing patient note de-identification systems should be performed using structured information from the EHRs, the latter being available in a typical, real-life setting. We restricted our EHR-derived features to patient and doctor names, but it could be extended to the many other structured fields that EHR contain, such as patients' addresses, phone numbers, email addresses, professions, and ages.

Acknowledgements

The project was supported by Philips Research. The content is solely the responsibility of the authors and does not necessarily represent the official views of Philips Research. We warmly thank Michele Filannino, Alistair Johnson, Li-wei Lehman, Roger Mark, and Tom Pollard for their helpful suggestions and technical assistance.

References

John Aberdeen, Samuel Bayer, Reyyan Yeniterzi, Ben Wellner, Cheryl Clark, David Hanauer, Bradley Malin, and Lynette Hirschman. 2010. The MITRE Identification Scrubber Toolkit: design, training, and assessment. *International journal of medical informatics*, 79(12):849–859.

Bruce A Beckwith, Rajeshwarri Mahaadevan, Ulysses J Balis, and Frank Kuo. 2006. Development and evaluation of an open source software tool for deidentification of pathology reports. *BMC medical informatics and decision making*, 6(1):1.

Jules J Berman. 2003. Concept-match medical data scrubbing: how pathology text can be used in research. *Archives of pathology & laboratory medicine*, 127(6):680–686.

Franck Dernoncourt, Ji Young Lee, Ozlem Uzuner, and Peter Szolovits. 2016. De-identification of patient notes with recurrent neural networks. *arXiv preprint arXiv:1606.03475*.

Catherine M DesRoches, Chantal Worzala, and Scott Bates. 2013. Some hospitals are falling behind in meeting meaningful use criteria and could be vulnerable to penalties in 2015. *Health Affairs*, 32(8):1355–1360.

Margaret Douglas, Gari Clifford, Andrew Reisner, George Moody, and Roger Mark. 2004. Computer-assisted de-identification of free text in the mimic ii database. In *Computers in Cardiology, 2004*, pages 341–344. IEEE.

Margaret Douglass, Gari Cliffford, Andrew Reisner, William Long, George Moody, and Roger Mark. 2005. De-identification algorithm for free-text nursing notes. In *Computers in Cardiology, 2005*, pages 331–334. IEEE.

Elliot M. Fielstein, Steven H. Brown, and Theodore Speroff. 2004. Algorithmic de-identification of VA medical exam text for HIPAA privacy compliance: Preliminary findings. *Medinfo*, 1590.

Michele Filannino and Goran Nenadic. 2015. Temporal expression extraction with extensive feature type selection and a posteriori label adjustment. *Data & Knowledge Engineering*, 100:19–33.

Jeff Friedlin and Clement J McDonald. 2008. A software tool for removing patient identifying information from clinical documents. *Journal of the American Medical Informatics Association*, 15(5):601–610.

Ary L Goldberger, Luis AN Amaral, Leon Glass, Jeffrey M Hausdorff, Plamen Ch Ivanov, Roger G Mark, Joseph E Mietus, George B Moody, Chung-Kang Peng, and H Eugene Stanley. 2000. Physiobank, physiotoolkit, and physionet components of a new research resource for complex physiologic signals. *Circulation*, 101(23):e215–e220.

Yikun Guo, Robert Gaizauskas, Ian Roberts, George Demetriou, and Mark Hepple. 2006. Identifying personal health information using support vector machines. In *i2b2 workshop on challenges in natural language processing for clinical data*, pages 10–11.

Dilip Gupta, Melissa Saul, and John Gilbertson. 2004. Evaluation of a deidentification (De-Id) software engine to share pathology reports and clinical documents for research. *American journal of clinical pathology*, 121(2):176–186.

Kazuo Hara. 2006. Applying a SVM based chunker and a text classifier to the deid challenge. In *i2b2 Workshop on challenges in natural language processing for clinical data*, pages 10–11. Am Med Inform Assoc.

Sepp Hochreiter and Jürgen Schmidhuber. 1997. Long short-term memory. *Neural computation*, 9(8):1735–1780.

Chun-Ju Hsiao, Esther Hing, Thomas C Socey, and Bill Cai. 2011. Electronic health record systems and intent to apply for meaningful use incentives among office-based physician practices: United states, 2001–2011. *system*, 18(17.3):17–3.

Alistair EW Johnson, Tom J Pollard, Lu Shen, Li-wei H Lehman, Mengling Feng, Mohammad Ghassemi, Benjamin Moody, Peter Szolovits, Leo Anthony Celi, and Roger G Mark. 2016. Mimic-iii, a freely accessible critical care database. *Scientific data*, 3.

Erin McCann. 2015. EHR vendor marketshare and MU attestations by vendor. *Healthcare IT News*.

Stephane M Meystre, F Jeffrey Friedlin, Brett R South, Shuying Shen, and Matthew H Samore. 2010. Automatic de-identification of textual documents in the electronic health record: a review of recent research. *BMC medical research methodology*, 10(1):1.

Frances P Morrison, Li Li, Albert M Lai, and George Hripcsak. 2009. Repurposing the clinical record: can an existing natural language processing system de-identify clinical notes? *Journal of the American Medical Informatics Association*, 16(1):37–39.

Ishna Neamatullah, Margaret Douglass, H Lehman Li-wei, Andrew Reisner, Mauricio Villarroel, William J Long, Peter Szolovits, George B Moody, Roger G Mark, and Gari D Clifford. 2008. Automated de-identification of free-text medical records. *BMC medical informatics and decision making*, 8(1):1.

HHS Office for Civil Rights. 2002. Standards for privacy of individually identifiable health information. final rule. *Federal Register*, 67(157):53181.

Robert Parker, David Graff, Junbo Kong, Ke Chen, and Kazuaki Maeda. 2011. English gigaword fifth edition, linguistic data consortium. Technical report, Technical Report. Linguistic Data Consortium, Philadelphia.

Jeffrey Pennington, Richard Socher, and Christopher D Manning. 2014. GloVe: global vectors for word representation. *Proceedings of the Empiricial Methods in Natural Language Processing (EMNLP 2014)*, 12:1532–1543.

Patrick Ruch, Robert H Baud, Anne-Marie Rassinoux, Pierrette Bouillon, and Gilbert Robert. 2000. Medical document anonymization with a semantic lexicon. In *Proceedings of the AMIA Symposium*, page 729. American Medical Informatics Association.

Mohammed Saeed, Mauricio Villarroel, Andrew T Reisner, Gari Clifford, Li-Wei Lehman, George Moody, Thomas Heldt, Tin H Kyaw, Benjamin Moody, and Roger G Mark. 2011. Multiparameter intelligent monitoring in intensive care II (MIMIC-II): a public-access intensive care unit database. *Critical care medicine*, 39(5):952.

Brett R South, Danielle Mowery, Ying Suo, Jianwei Leng, Óscar Ferrández, Stephane M Meystre, and Wendy W Chapman. 2014. Evaluating the effects of machine pre-annotation and an interactive annotation interface on manual de-identification of clinical text. *Journal of biomedical informatics*, 50:162–172.

Amber Stubbs, Christopher Kotfila, and Özlem Uzuner. 2015. Automated systems for the de-identification of longitudinal clinical narratives: Overview of 2014 i2b2/UTHealth shared task track 1. *Journal of biomedical informatics*, 58:S11–S19.

Latanya Sweeney. 1996. Replacing personally-identifying information in medical records, the Scrub system. In *Proceedings of the AMIA annual fall symposium*, page 333. American Medical Informatics Association.

György Szarvas, Richárd Farkas, and András Kocsor. 2006. A multilingual named entity recognition system using boosting and c4.5 decision tree learning algorithms. In *Discovery Science*, pages 267–278. Springer.

Sean M Thomas, Burke Mamlin, Gunther Schadow, and Clement McDonald. 2002. A successful technique for removing names in pathology reports using an augmented search and replace method. In *Proceedings of the AMIA Symposium*, page 777. American Medical Informatics Association.

Özlem Uzuner, Tawanda C Sibanda, Yuan Luo, and Peter Szolovits. 2008. A de-identifier for medical discharge summaries. *Artificial intelligence in medicine*, 42(1):13–35.

Adam Wright, Stanislav Henkin, Joshua Feblowitz, Allison B McCoy, David W Bates, and Dean F Sittig. 2013. Early results of the meaningful use program for electronic health records. *New England Journal of Medicine*, 368(8):779–780.

Hui Yang and Jonathan M Garibaldi. 2015. Automatic detection of protected health information from clinic narratives. *Journal of biomedical informatics*, 58:S30–S38.

Semi-supervised Clustering of Medical Text

Pracheta Sahoo
Dept. of Computer Science
University of Texas at Dallas
pracheta.sahoo@utdallas.edu

Asif Ekbal and **Sriparna Saha**
Dept. of Computer Science
and Engineering
IIT Patna, Bihta
asif,sriparna@iitp.ac.in

Diego Mollá
Dept. of Computing
Macquarie University
Sydney, Australia
diego.molla-aliod@mq.edu.au

Kaushik Nandan
Dept. of Computer Science
and Engineering
IIT Patna, Bihta
kaushalta@gmail.com

Abstract

Semi-supervised clustering is an attractive alternative for traditional (unsupervised) clustering in targeted applications. By using the information of a small annotated dataset, semi-supervised clustering can produce clusters that are customized to the application domain. In this paper, we present a semi-supervised clustering technique based on a multi-objective evolutionary algorithm (NSGA-II-clus). We apply this technique to the task of clustering medical publications for Evidence Based Medicine (EBM) and observe an improvement of the results against unsupervised and other semi-supervised clustering techniques.

1 Introduction

Clustering is an unsupervised machine learning method that attempts to find groups (clusters) in a collection of documents (Jain et al., 1999). Clustering is useful for applications where the goal is to find structure in a collection of documents, and can be applied in a wide range of tasks, such as finding groups among patients with breast cancer, or identifying groups of shoppers with similar browsing and purchase histories. A common problem with clustering, however, is that the structure that is found might not reflect the desired structure that is relevant for a particular application. For example, one might wish to cluster words in the hope of learning their parts-of-speech, but instead the clusters group words according to their meanings. In supervised learning, we have labeled information, but the annotation can be costly to produce (Zhu and Goldberg, 2009). So a trade-off is needed, and a semi-supervised framework provides this trade-off. In semi-supervised clustering (Zhu and Goldberg, 2009), part of the documents to cluster are annotated with information about how they cluster, and the task consists of clustering the entire set of documents. By incorporating the information of the known clusters of a part of the documents, the final clusters have a better chance to match the desired clusters of the application domain. In this paper we focus on clustering the documents that are relevant to a clinical query for the practice of Evidence Based Medicine (EBM) (Shash and Molla, 2013). Here, each cluster is expected to group the documents that describe a particular aspect of the answer to the clinical question. Let us take an example of the disease Asperger's syndrome. There are five policies for the treatment of this disease, namely 'special education', 'behavior modification', 'speech', 'physical and occupational therapy and medication', and 'social skill therapies and medications'. Now the documents which are assigned to each of these possible treatment policies represent a cluster. Table 1 shows an example of such clustering. Moreover, Table 1 shows that some documents may be associated with multiple treatments, and therefore the clustering task is non-overlapping.

Most of the clustering techniques in existing literature focus on optimizing only one validity index (Jain et al., 1999; Maulik and Bandyopadhyay, 2002), which measures the goodness of an obtained par-

23

Proceedings of the Clinical Natural Language Processing Workshop,
pages 23–31, Osaka, Japan, December 11-17 2016.

Table 1: Asperger's syndrome and its possible treatments. Each item enclosed in [] indicates a text document ID.

Which treatments work best for Asperger's syndrome?	
Name of the treatment	IDs of documents assigned
Special education	[1080], [1178]
Behavior modification	[8545], [4123], [5523]
Speech, physical or occupational therapy	[1080], [8545]
Social skills therapies	[5523], [3321], [6434]
Medications	[8545], [3321], [6434], [6755]

titioning. However, in order to determine a proper partitioning, optimizing a single cluster validity index is not always sufficient, especially in the situation when we deal with text documents having clusters of different shapes and sizes. The concept of multi-objective optimization (MOO) can be brought into consideration where we need to optimize several objective functions at the same time. The advantage of MOO is that we can generate clusters by optimizing several cluster validity indices. Inspired by this, Ekbal et al. (2013) proposed a MOO-based approach for clustering medical documents for EBM by using the search capability of a simulated annealing based approach, AMOSA (Archived MultiObjective Simulated Annealing based technique) (Bandyopadhyay et al., 2008). However, it has been shown that for some benchmark datasets, AMOSA performs slowly compared to a popular genetic algorithm based MOO technique, NSGA-II (Non-dominated Sorting Genetic Algorithm-II) (Bandyopadhyay et al., 2008). Therefore, an alternative MOO-based approach is needed in order to verify whether we can improve the run-time complexity of AMOSA. Moreover, Ekbal et al. (2013) have used some labeled information to select a single solution from the final set of trade-off solutions. In general semi-supervised methods perform well compared to unsupervised clustering techniques.

In our present work we propose to develop a semi-supervised clustering technique and apply that for EBM. The proposed approach uses only 10% labeled information which is easy to obtain. The proposed technique is novel in a way that it uses the labeled information during the internal steps of the proposed clustering process. More specifically we can say that the internal steps of NSGA-II based clustering are modified to take care of this labeled information. The labeled information was used by Ekbal et al. (2013) to select a single solution from the final Pareto optimal front after the execution of AMOSA based clustering technique. Moreover, as mentioned by Bandyopadhyay et al. (2008), the complexity of AMOSA is higher than that of NSGA-II. Thus, the use of NSGA-II as the underlying optimization technique makes the system less complex and time consuming. In this paper, we propose the use of NSGA-II (Deb et al., 2013) for semi-supervised clustering of documents. We propose two different versions of the NSGA-II based semi-supervised clustering technique. In the first approach the available supervised information in the form of must-link and cannot-link constraints can be used during the selection phase of clustering. These constraints are taken into account while calculating crowding distance which is further used to assign ranks to different solutions of the combined population. Thus, the available supervised information is used in each generation of the proposed technique. In the second approach, we use a semi-supervised approach to select a single solution from the set of final solutions produced by the MOO-based approach. In this case, supervised information is used only at the final stage rather than during the clustering phase. In recent years, several semi-supervised clustering techniques (Xing et al., 2002; Basu et al., 2004) have been proposed in the literature which are applicable for general data sets. In this paper we also extend those techniques to solve the problem of EBM. Some of the promising methods include the ones based on K-means with a distance metric (Xing et al., 2002) and K-means with a probabilistic framework (Basu et al., 2004). We, thereafter, present a thorough comparative analysis with our proposed methods and other existing semi-supervised clustering techniques.

2 Background

In this section we describe some concepts related to multi-objective optimization (MOO).

2.1 MultiObjective Optimization

Simultaneously optimizing several objective functions is known as multi-Objective optimization (MOO) (Deb, 2001). In general the objective functions used in MOO are conflicting in nature. A real-life example could be buying a car where the objectives are : i) minimizing cost and ii) maximizing comfort. In mathematical terms, a MOO problem can be formally stated as: Finding the vectors of decision variables $x = [x_1, x_2, x_3, \ldots\ldots, x_n]^T$ which will satisfy m inequality constraints: $g_i(x) \geq 0, i = 1, 2, \ldots. m$ and p equality constraints $h_j(x) = 0, j = 1, 2, \ldots, p$ and simultaneously optimize M objective functions $f_1(x), f_2(x), \ldots., f_M(x)$.

2.2 Domination

A solution $x^i = \{f_1(x^i), f_2(x^i), \ldots, f_M(x^i)\}$ is said to dominate a solution $x^j = \{f_1(x^j), f_2(x^j), \ldots, f_M(x^j)\}$ denoted as $x^i \prec x^j$ iff $f_m(x^i) < f_m(x^j)$, $\exists m \in \{1, 2, \ldots, M\}$, and $f_m(x^i) \leq f_m(x^j)$, $\forall m \in \{1, 2, \ldots, M\}$

Two solutions x^i and x^j are said to be non-dominated with each other if and only if neither $x^i \prec x^j$ nor $x^j \prec x^i$.

A solution $x \in P$ is called *Pareto Optimal* with respect to P if there is no solution $x' \in P$ such that x is dominated by x'. The set of Pareto Optimal solutions is known as *Pareto set*.

Non Dominated Sorting is to divide the population $\mathbb{P}$ in $K(1 \leq K \leq N)$ fronts. Let $\mathcal{F} = \{F_1, F_2, \ldots, F_K\}$ be the set of these K fronts in decreasing order of their dominance. The division of the solutions is such that i) Each solution in a front is non-dominated with each other, and ii) each solution in a front F_k is dominated by at least one solution in its preceding front $F_{k'}, k' < k \bigwedge 1 \leq k, k' \leq K$.

2.3 NSGA-II in the Light of MOO

Solving a problem consisting of multiple objectives in general produces more than one solution and these obtained solutions are termed as Pareto Optimal solutions. If no external condition is specified, it becomes really difficult to distinguish between these sets of solutions in terms of their performance. In the current state-of-art, we have always observed a tendency to convert the MOO problem into a single objective optimization (SOO) problem in order to produce single Pareto optimal solution at a time.

In this regard, a number of multiObjective-based evolutionary algorithms (MOEA) have been proposed (Deb, 2001; Fonseca and Fleming, 1993), where the algorithm deals with a number of competing objectives simultaneously. NSGA (Tanaka et al., 1995) is one of such members in the league of suggested EA (Evolutionary Algorithms) methods. NSGA-II (Deb et al., 2013) is an improvement over the existing NSGA algorithm, where a diverse set of solutions is found and it is observed that the algorithm tends to converge near the true Pareto optimal set. Among all such existing EAs, NSGA-II performs better than the rest and hence it is a promising algorithm for EA based MOO.

3 NSGA-II-Based Clustering Algorithm

In this section we describe the basic framework of NSGA-II-based clustering approach. The proposed clustering technique can detect the number of clusters automatically.

3.1 Problem Encoding

In this algorithm, cluster medoids are encoded in the form of a chromosome. We therefore assume that the medoid is the most representative point of a given cluster. The number of clusters is varied over a range, 2 to K_{max} where K_{max} is the maximum possible number of clusters. So for a given chromosome, first a random number is generated in the range of 2 to K_{max}. Let this be K_i. The K_i centers are encoded in that particular chromosome and those centers are randomly chosen from the set of all documents. Each document is assigned a positive integer value at the beginning. A point in the chromosome represents any such document. But all the values within the chromosome must be unique, that is there should not be any repetition while assigning values *i.e.*, document IDs in the chromosome should be unique. At first the population is initialized randomly. If the length of the population is p, we will generate p chromosomes at the beginning. For example, suppose we have 9 documents having IDs from 0 to 9 and the K_i value is 4. Let us assume that the initial selection of documents for the medoids have IDs 2, 6, 7 and 9. The chromosome becomes (**2 6 7 9**).

3.2 Assignment of Documents to Different Clusters

In our experiments we have used cosine and Euclidean distance as separate parameters to assign the documents in respective clusters. For each document we determine any of the available distance measures with respect to all the cluster medoids (encoded in a particular chromosome). Finally the document is assigned to that cluster medoid ($\overline{m}_i$) with respect to which it is having the minimum distance. Once the assignment has been done for all the documents, the new cluster medoids are calculated based on the new clusters formed. These new medoids replace the existing medoids represented in that particular chromosome.

$$j = \arg \min_{j=1}^{K} d(\overline{x}, \overline{m}_j).$$

Here, $\overline{x}$ represents a document and $\overline{m}_j$ denotes the jth cluster-medoid. The function $d(\overline{x}, \overline{m}_j)$ represents any distance measure between document $\overline{x}$ and cluster medoid $\overline{m}_j$. The document $\overline{x}$ would be finally assigned to cluster j. Once the assignment has been done for all the documents, the new cluster medoids are calculated based on the new clusters formed. These new medoids replace the existing medoids represented in that particular chromosome.

3.3 Objective Functions Used

Several cluster validity indices exist in the literature like: Davies-Bouldin (DB) index (Davies and Bouldin, 1979), Dunns index (Dunn, 1973), Calinski Harabasz index (Caliński and Harabasz, 1974), Xie-Beni (XB) index (Xie and Beni, 1991), I-index (Maulik and Bandyopadhyay, 2002). These indices can measure the goodness of an obtained partitioning. It is established by Maulik and Bandyopadhyay (2002) that I-index performs better than the existing cluster validity indices in terms of finding the appropriate number of clusters. Hence, in order to measure the goodness of the partitioning represented in a particular chromosome, two cluster validity indices are used, I-index (Maulik and Bandyopadhyay, 2002) and XB index (Xie and Beni, 1991).

3.4 Genetic Operators

We use classical mutation and crossover operators as proposed in NSGA-II (Deb et al., 2013) to bring diversity in our population. Suppose there is a chromosome (2 4 5 7 8 9) representing a parent chromosome. In a mutation two documents are selected and exchanged.

(2 **4** 5 7 8 **9**) => (2 **9** 5 7 8 **4**)

In the case of crossover operation the bits are exchanged between parent chromosomes to produce off-springs. Once a crossover point is selected, the permutation till this point is copied from the first parent, then the second parent is scanned and, if the number is not yet in the offspring, it is added. For example, suppose the parent chromosomes are represented by (1 2 3 4 5 6 7 8 9) and (4 5 3 6 8 9 7 2 1) and the crossover point is 5. The offspring becomes :

(**1 2 3 4 5** 6 7 8 9) + (4 5 3 6 8 9 7 2 1) => (1 2 3 4 5 6 8 9 7)

Thereafter the selection operation of NSGA-II is applied. As described in (Deb et al., 2013), first the old population and the new population obtained after the application of mutation and crossover are merged. Now the non-dominated sorting procedure of NSGA-II is applied to divide the merged population (if the population size is N, then the size of the merged population is $2 \times N$) into a set of non-dominated fronts. The selection operation is illustrated in Fig 2. Solutions belonging to the best non-dominated set F_1 are among the best solutions in the combined population. If the size of F_1 is smaller than N, all members of the set are selected for the new population. The remaining members of the population are chosen from subsequent non-dominated fronts in the order of their ranking. If for a particular front F_i, $\|F_i\| > (N - \sum_{j=1}^{i-1} \|F_j\|)$, then all the solutions of the F_i front cannot be accommodated in the new population. In that case, in order to select the required number of solutions, the concept of crowding distance is used. In order to ensure diversity, the solutions which are far away lying in some non-crowded region are given special attention. Those are given higher priority while being selected.

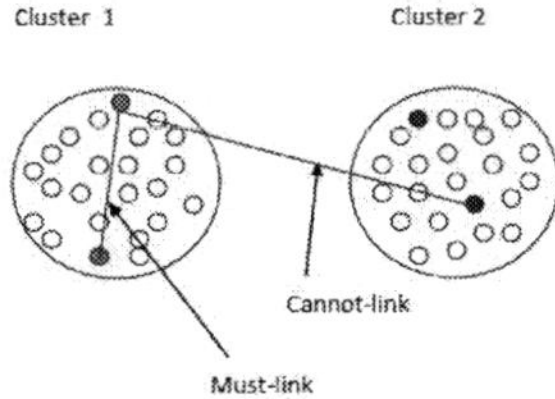

Figure 1: Concepts of must-link and cannot-link constriants

Until the limit is reached, iterations are performed and the steps of mutation, crossover and selection are repeated. Finally, a set of non-dominated solutions on the final Pareto front is obtained.

4 Application of Semi-supervision on NSGA-II Algorithm

As mentioned earlier we have used two different methods to induce the flavor of semi-supervision in NSGA-II algorithm. These methods are described below:

4.0.1 Internal-NSGA-II-clus

Here we perform some modifications in the selection step of NSGA-II to take care of the available supervised information in terms of must-link and cannot-link constraints. The computation of non-dominated fronts depends not only on the objective functions (XB and I indices) but on the available constraints (must-link, cannot-link) also. Here, the number of constraints violated by each solution also contributes in determining the rank of that solution during selection operation.

A must-link constraint ensures that two instances should remain in the same cluster as shown in Fig 1, whereas a cannot-link constraint ensures that two instances should be in two different clusters. From the initial labeled information the must-link and cannot-link constraints are chosen. It is assumed that the documents lying in the same cluster obey must-link and the documents lying in different clusters obey cannot-link.

Along with XB and I indices, 10% of the labeled information in the form of must-link and cannot link constraints is also used in crowded distance computation.

4.1 Computation of Crowding Distance

If n is the number of solutions in a given front F, $F(d_j)$ is the crowding distance of jth solution at a given front F, and $I(d_1)$ and $I(d_n)$ are boundary values for crowding distance in F, then the procedure through which the crowding distance is calculated is described in Algorithm 1, where $I(k).m$ is the mth

Algorithm 1 Computation of crowding distance

1: **for** each front F **do**
2:    $F(d_j) = 0$
3:    **for** each objective function m **do**
4:       sort the individuals in F based on m, such that
5:       $I = sort(F, m)$
6:       $F(d_1) = \infty$ and $F(d_n) = \infty$.
7:       **for** $k = 2$ to $(n-1)$ **do**
8:          $F(d_k) = F(d_k) + \frac{I(k+1).m - I(k-1).m}{f_m^{max} - f_m^{min}}$
9:       **end for**
10:   **end for**
11: **end for**

---

objective function of the kth individual in I, f_m^{max} is the maximum value of m th objective function, and f_m^{min} is the minimum value of mth objective function.

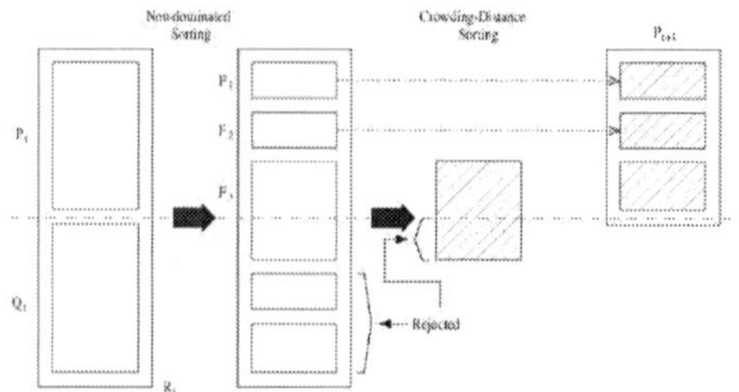

Figure 2: Selection operation of NSGA-II

4.2 Modified Crowding Distance

Along with the available objective functions, we also consider the available must-link and cannot-link constraints while computing the crowding distance. For a given solution (S), its must-score (w_m) and cannot-score (w_c) are calculated. If S obeys a must-link constraint then its must-score is increased by 1 whereas if it obeys a cannot-link constraint then its cannot-score is increased by 1.

The overall must-score w_m of an individual solution (S) is calculated as follows: $w_m = \sum_{i=1}^{M} I_{f_M^i}$

$$I_{f_M^i} = 1 \quad , \quad \text{if } S \text{ satisfies the } i\text{th must-link} \tag{1}$$
$$= 0 \quad , \quad \text{otherwise} \tag{2}$$

Here M: total number of must-links, f_M^i represents ith must-link constraint. Similarly, cannot-score w_c of an individual solution is calculated as follows: $w_c = \sum_{i=1}^{C} I_{f_C^i}$

$$I_{f_C^i} = 1 \quad , \quad \text{if } S \text{ satisfies the } i\text{th cannot-link} \tag{3}$$
$$= 0 \quad , \quad \text{otherwise} \tag{4}$$

Here C: total number of cannot-links, f_C^i represents ith cannot-link constraint.

The modified crowding distance of kth solution is computed as follows.
$$F(dnew_k) = F(d_k) + \frac{w_m}{M} + \frac{w_c}{C}$$
where $F(d_k)$ is the original crowding distance of kth solution computed using the procedure mentioned in Section 4.1. And w_m and w_c are the total must-score and cannot-score of kth solution, respectively.

Selection After the computation of crowding distance the selection process is carried out using the crowded-comparison operator $(\prec_n)$ (Deb et al., 2013). Let us assume that $F(dnew_j)$ corresponds to the new crowding distance for the jth individual in non-dominated front F and p and q are the pth and q^{th} individuals of a particular non dominated front F. After the application of the non-dominated sorting procedure, suppose solutions p and q are assigned ranks of p_{rank} and q_{rank}, respectively. Then the crowded-comparison operator is defined as follows in Algorithm 2.

Algorithm 2 Computation of crowded comparison operator

$p \prec_n q$ (q dominates p) if
i) $p_{rank} < q_{rank}$ or ii) if $p_{rank} = q_{rank}$, i.e. p and $q \in F$ then $F(dnew_p) > F(dnew_q)$ $i.e.$, the crowding distance should be greater.

4.3 External-NSGA-II-clus

In this method, at first the unsupervised clustering technique NSGA-II-clus (as described in Section 3) is executed on the given set of documents to obtain different partitionings on the final Pareto front. Here no modification is done in the internal steps of NSGA-II-clus, the available supervised information is used to select a single best solution from the final non-dominated set of solutions. 10% information in the form of must-link and cannot-link constraints is used to rank each of the non-dominated set of solutions. Basically each solution on the final Pareto front represents a partitioning. Experiments are performed to check which partitioning obeys the available must-link and cannot-link information. The solution with the maximum match is selected as the final solution from the Pareto Optimal front. For each solution on the final Pareto front, we follow some scoring mechanism. For must-links, if two points present in the link lie in the same cluster present in that solution, then we increase the score of the solution by 1. Similarly, for cannot-links, if two points present in the link lie in two different clusters, we increase the score of the non-dominated solution by 1. Thus we calculate the scores of all non-dominated solutions. The solution with the highest score is selected as the final solution.

5 Datasets and Experimental Results

We use the dataset made available by Mollá and Santiago-Martinez (2011), from which we randomly extract 276 clinical questions. Each question is associated with an average of 5.89 documents, and can be seen as an independent clustering task. The proposed NSGA-II-clus (internal and external) and AMOSA-clus (Ekbal et al., 2013) clustering techniques are therefore applied on each question individually. The average entropy value of all the questions is then calculated. For both internal and external NSGA-II clus algorithm, we first select 10% of the must-link and cannot-link constraints. For Internal-NSGA-II-clus, this supervised information is used in providing ranking of all the solutions during selection phase of each generation. In case of External-NSGA-II-clus this available supervised information is used in assigning a score to each of the solutions on the final Pareto front. Based on the highest score we select a single solution and compute the entropy values accordingly. The parameters for the proposed NSGA-II-clus (internal and external) semi-supervised approach are as follows: population size = 20, number of generations = 20, mutation probability = 0.2 and crossover probability = 0.6. These values were determined after performing a thorough sensitivity study. The parameters of AMOSA-clus are kept similar to those reported by Ekbal et al. (2013).The proposed NSGA-II-clus (internal and external) and AMOSA-clus approaches along with two semi-supervised approaches, namely K-Means with Distance Metric (Xing et al., 2002) and K-Means with probabilistic framework (Basu et al., 2004) are applied on the same datasets.

The K-Means+ Distance Metric (Xing et al., 2002) algorithm in its simplest sense is a variation of K-means. In the usual K-means, Euclidean or cosine distance is used as a measure of distance or separation between any two points in the space. Suppose an user wants certain points to be regarded as similar, according to some distance metric. Our task is to learn a distance metric automatically over a set of points which takes into account this relationship. In this algorithm, however instead of Euclidean or cosine distance, the concept of Distance Metric is used for our benefit.[1]

In the case of a probabilistic framework, a set of data points is randomly partitioned into a specific number of clusters which serve as the unsupervised partitioning initially. Here also supervision is provided in terms of two constraints *i.e.*, must-link and cannot-link (Basu et al., 2004). A modified version of Expectation-Maximization algorithm is used here to obtain the final partitioning which also obeys the available supervised information.

Table 2: Cluster entropies obtained by different approaches. Here KM_{DM} and KM_{Prob} denote, respectively, the *K*-means with distance-metric-based approach and *K*-means with probabilistic approach

Dist.	*AMOSA*		*Internal NSGA-II*		*External NSGA-II*		KM_{DM}	KM_{Prob}
	best	average	best	average	best	average		
Euclidean	0.177	0.235	0.025	0.092	0.063	0.117	0.534	0.274
Cosine	0.177	0.230	0.018	0.067	0.070	0.122	—	0.296

---

[1]To simplify our terminology, in this paper we use the term "cosine distance" to represent 1 - cosine similarity. The fact that neither the cosine distance nor the cosine similarity are true distance metrics does not affect the argumentation in this paper.

Two versions of the proposed NSGA-II-clus (internal and external) and AMOSA-clus algorithms are executed with the following distance measures: i) (version 1) Euclidean distance as the similarity measure for the assignment of documents to different clusters and also for the computation of objective functions; and ii) (version 2) with cosine similarity as the similarity measure for the assignment of documents to different clusters and also for the computation of objective functions. The average entropy values attained by these techniques are reported in Table 2. For the best-case computation we select those solutions from the final Pareto front obtained by internal-NSGA-II-clus and AMOSA-clus which possess the minimum entropy values. In the case of external-NSGA-II-clus, the best solution is selected using the steps as discussed in Section 4.3. The corresponding entropy values for those solutions are calculated. For the average case (unsupervised) computation we select all the solutions on the final Pareto Optimal front and calculate entropy for each of the solutions. Then we take the average entropy of all the solutions and report those values both for NSGA-II-clus (internal and external) and AMOSA-clus in Table 2.

Table 2 shows that, using 10% supervised information, the probabilistic framework approach outperforms the distance metric learning approach in case of Euclidean distance measure. Among all the algorithms, semi-supervised internal-NSGA-II-clus yields the highest performance in the best case as well as in the average case. This is also better than the AMOSA-based clustering algorithm, which was used for EBM by Ekbal et al. (2013). In order to show that our proposed NSGA-II-clus (internal and external) is also able to predict the correct number of clusters from different questions automatically, we have reported the error rate as below: $error = \frac{\sum_i (target_i - predicted_i)^2}{\#of questions}$

Here $target_i$ denotes the actual number of clusters for a particular question and $predicted_i$ denotes the predicted number of clusters by the proposed NSGA-II-clus (internal and external) technique for a particular question. Here as mentioned earlier in Section 2, for each question, we have varied the number of clusters in the range 2 to $\sqrt{n}$ where n is the number of documents per question. The average number of clusters identified by the proposed Internal-NSGA-II-clus optimizing XB-index and I-index as the objective functions for each question are 2.13 and 2.27, respectively, with cosine and Euclidean distance measurements. The average number of clusters identified by the proposed external-NSGA-II-clus optimizing XB-index and I-index as the objective functions for each question are 2.45 and 2.32, respectively, with cosine and Euclidean distance measurements. The average number of clusters in the actual annotated set is 2.38. Moreover we have also computed the error rates of different automatic clustering techniques. For AMOSA-clus the error rates are 1.90 with cosine similarity and 1.91 with Euclidean distance. For internal-NSGA-II-clus the error rates are 1.33 with cosine similarity and 1.49 with Euclidean distance. For External-NSGA-II-clus the error rates are 1.74 with cosine similarity and 1.69 with Euclidean distance. In Ref. (Ekbal et al., 2013) it has already been proved that AMOSA-clus provides the minimal error rate compared to different existing techniques and heuristics. But the proposed approach provides minimal error rate compared to AMOSA-clus. This again proves the efficacy of the proposed semi-supervised approach.

6   Conclusion

In this paper we have used semi-supervised clustering to find clusters of medical publications for the task of Evidence Based Medicine. We have proposed two different frameworks using the concepts of MultiObjective Optimization (MOO) for solving the problem of semi-supervised clustering. As the underlying optimization technique we have used a popular evolutionary strategy, NSGA-II. A comparative study between two MOO-based semi-supervised clustering approaches and two existing semi-supervised approaches is also provided. Our experiments show the efficacy of the MOO-based semi-supervised approach on medical publications. The improved results using several objective functions are encouraging. The comparative study on medical data proves the efficacy of our NSGA-II based approach. In future, we would like to compare the proposed technique with alternative supervised techniques. We wish to explore other similarity measures to determine the distance between two given documents. The proposed technique would also be evaluated on other data sets and non-overlapping clustering techniques.

References

Sanghamitra Bandyopadhyay, Sriparna Saha, Ujjwal Maulik, and Kalyanmoy Deb. 2008. A simulated annealing-based multiobjective optimization algorithm: Amosa. *IEEE Transactions on Evolutionary Computation*, 12(3):269–283, June.

Sugato Basu, Mikhail Bilenko, and Raymond J. Mooney. 2004. A probabilistic framework for semi-supervised clustering. *Proceedings of the Tenth ACM SIGKDD International Conference on Knowledge Discovery and Data Mining(KDD 2004*, pages 59–68, August.

Tadeusz Caliński and Jerzy Harabasz. 1974. A dendrite method for cluster analysis. *Communications in Statistics-theory and Methods*, (1):1–27.

David L. Davies and Donald W. Bouldin. 1979. A cluster separation measure. *IEEE transactions on pattern analysis and machine intelligence*, pages 224–227.

Kalyanmoy Deb, Amrit Pratap, Sameer Agarwal, and T. Meyarivan. 2013. A fast and elitist multiobjective genetic algorithm: Nsga-II. *Artificial Intelligence in Medicine. Springer Berlin Heidelberg*, pages 305–309.

K. Deb. 2001. Multi-objective optimization using evolutionary algorithms. *John Wiley & Sons*.

Joseph C Dunn. 1973. A fuzzy relative of the isodata process and its use in detecting compact well-separated clusters. pages 32–57.

Asif Ekbal, Sriparna Saha, Diego Molla, and K Ravikumar. 2013. Multi-objective optimization for clustering of medical publications. *Proceedings of the Australasian Language Technology Association Workshop 2013 (ALTA 2013)*, pages 53–61, December.

Carlos M. Fonseca and Peter J. Fleming. 1993. Genetic algorithms for multiobjective optimization: Formulation, discussion and generalization. *ICGA*.

Anil K. Jain, M. Narasimha Murty, and Patrick J. Flynn. 1999. Data clustering: a review. *ACM computing surveys (CSUR)*, 31(3):264–323.

U. Maulik and S. Bandyopadhyay. 2002. Performance evaluation of some clustering algorithms and validity indices. *Pattern Analysis and Machine Intelligence, IEEE Transactions*, 24(12):1650–1654.

Diego Mollá and Maria Elena Santiago-Martinez. 2011. Development of a corpus for evidence based medicine summarisation. *Proceedings of the Australasian Language Technology Association Workshop*.

Sara Faisal Shash and Diego Molla. 2013. Clustering of medical publications for evidence based medicine summarisation. *Artificial Intelligence in Medicine. Springer Berlin Heidelberg*, pages 305–309.

Masahiro Tanaka, Hikaru Watanabe, Yasuyuki Furukawa, and Tetsuzo Tanino. 1995. Ga-based decision support system for multicriteria optimization. *Systems, Man and Cybernetics, 1995. Intelligent Systems for the 21st Century., IEEE International Conference*, pages 1556–1561.

Xuanli Lisa Xie and Gerardo Beni. 1991. A validity measure for fuzzy clustering. *IEEE Transactions on pattern analysis and machine intelligence*, 13(8):841–847.

Eric P. Xing, Andrew Y. Ng, Michael I. Jordan, and Stuart Russel. 2002. Distance metric learning, with application to clustering with side-information. *In Advances in neural information processing systems*, pages 505–512.

Xiaojin Zhu and Andrew B. Goldberg. 2009. Introduction to semi-supervised learning. *Synthesis lectures on artificial intelligence and machine learning*, 3(1):1–130.

Deep Learning Architecture for Patient Data De-identification in Clinical Records

Shweta, Asif Ekbal, Sriparna Saha, Pushpak Bhattacharyya
Indian Institute of Technology Patna
Bihar, India
{shweta.pcs14,asif,sriparna,pb}@iitp.ac.in

Abstract

Rapid growth in Electronic Medical Records (EMR) has emerged to an expansion of data in the clinical domain. The majority of the available health care information is sealed in the form of narrative documents which form the rich source of clinical information. Text mining of such clinical records has gained huge attention in various medical applications like treatment and decision making. However, medical records enclose patient Private Health Information (PHI) which can reveal the identities of the patients. In order to retain the privacy of patients, it is mandatory to remove all the PHI information prior to making it publicly available. The aim is to de-identify or encrypt the PHI from the patient medical records. In this paper, we propose an algorithm based on deep learning architecture to solve this problem. We perform de-identification of seven PHI terms from the clinical records. Experiments on benchmark datasets show that our proposed approach achieves encouraging performance, which is better than the baseline model developed with Conditional Random Field.

1 Introduction

With the phenomenal growth in medical interpretation, there have been tremendous increase of Electronic Medical Records (EMR) (Beck et al., 2012). Clinical documents contain valuable information (patient disease, medical procedure applied and medication) which have resulted in drawing good attention of researchers to explore and extract relevant information from the clinical text. However, these medical records consist of patient Private Health Information (PHI) (e.g., Patient name, Age, Doctor name, ID, Phone number, Address etc.) which can reveal the patient identity during the course of treatment. To avoid disclosing PHI information, it is mandatory according to the Health Insurance Portability and Accountability Act (HIPAA)[1], 1996, that the PHI terms are required to be hidden and protected prior to making it publicly available. De-identification is, thus, defined as the process of identifying and hiding PHI from clinical records and maintaining the integrity as much as possible (Stubbs et al., 2015). While during the course of PHI identification for removal, it is highly necessary for a de-identification process to retain the medical contents of the records so that this information can help further research and conserve the value of the record. However, de-identifying the records manually is quite unfeasible and expensive both in terms of time, efforts and cost. As such there is a huge requirement for an automated de-identification system.

De-identification task can be, in general, looked up as a traditional Named Entity Recognition (NER) task. Basically, NER can be thought of as a sequence labeling task with the goal to identify proper output sequences of the entities. Therefore, for every input sequence of words, the best labeled-sequence is to be obtained. De-identification task can be, in general, looked up as a traditional Named Entity Recognition (NER) task with the goal to identify proper output sequences of the entities. Therefore, for every input sequence of tokens, the best labeled-sequence is to be obtained. De-identification poses several challenges (Meystre et al., 2008). The two major hurdles for identifying PHI terms are as follows:

---

[1]http://www.hhs.gov/hipaa

Proceedings of the Clinical Natural Language Processing Workshop,
pages 32–41, Osaka, Japan, December 11-17 2016.

(1) Inter-PHI ambiguity: The ambiguity problem, where due to the lexical similarity, PHI terms overlap with the non-PHI terms. Example includes *Brown* (Doctor name) which is a PHI term vs. *brown* which is a non-PHI term.

(2) Intra-PHI ambiguity: This problem appears when one candidate word seems to belong to two different PHI terms. For example, the word *August* which is a Patient name vs. *August* which also denotes the possible candidate for date expression.

The problem of patient data de-identification has been addressed very recently in the shared task, Center of Informatics for Integrating Biology (i2b2) challenge[2]. The existing systems of patient data de-identification can be classified under three categories *viz.* rule-based, machine learning based and hybrid technique. Rule-based system follows patterns based on regular expression and gazetteers identified by the human. In practice, the set of rules corresponding to a system are restricted to a particular domain. Generally, the system fails when the domain is altered. To overcome this drawback, machine learning approaches have been proposed and found to be very successful in solving this de-identification problem. Some of the popular machine learning models proposed include support vector machine (Hara, 2006), (Guo et al., 2006), decision tree (Szarvas et al., 2006), log-linear models and most used conditional random fields (CRFs)(Yang and Garibaldi, 2015; He et al., 2015). Supervised machine learning and rule-based approach share the following drawbacks: these techniques require the labeled data and prominent feature set or the rules. This incurs cost and time as the appropriate set of features or rules can be framed only after analyzing the full records.

The advent of deep learning algorithms has facilitated to introduce a new framework where we do not require handcrafted features or rules. These models have the abilities to learn automatically the relevant features by performing composition over the words represented in the form of vectors known as word embedding. In recent times, deep neural network architecture has shown promise for solving various NLP tasks such as text classification (Socher et al., 2013; Kim, 2014), language modeling (Mikolov et al., 2010), question answering (Weston et al., 2015), machine translation (Bahdanau et al., 2014), spoken language understanding (Mesnil et al., 2013) etc. In this paper, we propose a novel system (DI-RNN) based on deep learning for patient data de-identification (PDI). We formulate the task as a sequence labeling problem and develop a technique based on Recurrent Neural Network (RNN) (Mikolov et al., 2010). RNN, unlike other techniques, does not require features to be explicitly generated for classifier's training or testing. Instead it learns features by itself which makes this approach domain adaptable and scalable. We develop a system for PDI in line with the framework introduced in Center of Informatics for Integrating Biology and the Bedside (i2b2) challenge[3]. The goal of the task was to identify all the PHI terms from the medical records. Firstly, we develop a baseline model based on a supervised machine learning algorithm, namely conditional random field (CRF) (Lafferty et al., 2001). The classifier is trained with a set of features automatically extracted from the training documents. We implement and compare different variants of RNN architectures, such as Elman-type networks (Elman, 1990; Mikolov et al., 2011) and Jordan-type networks (Jordan, 1997). The main aim of our paper is to study the effectiveness of deep learning techniques over the traditional supervised approaches for de-identification task.

2   Patient Data De-identification Task

The problem of patient data de-identification can be thought as a task equivalent to named entity recognition (NER). The main aim of both the tasks is to automatically identify noun phrases or part of noun phrases from the text. The problem of de-identification can be modeled as a two-step process, where in the first step all the PHI terms are required to be identified and classified, and in the later stage, identified PHI terms are encrypted. Here, we provide an example sentence with the corresponding NEs highlighted. Here, the input is the sequence of words W and the output corresponds to the sequence of labels L corresponding to the word-sequence and the corresponding de-identified sentence as shown in Table-1. Traditionally, the task can be visualized as follows: for a given word sequence W, the aim is to

---

[2]https://www.i2b2.org/

[3]https://www.i2b2.org/

Sentence	To	follow	up	with	Dr.	John	D	Doe
Named Entity	O	O	O	O	O	B-DOCTOR	I-DOCTOR	I-DOCTOR

Table 1: Examples of PHI instances represented by 'BIO' notation

find the best possible label-sequence that has maximum posterior probability i.e., $P(L|W)$. The Bayes rule is applied in the case of generative model framework as

$$\hat{L} = argmax_L P(L|W)$$
$$= argmax_L P(W|L)P(L) \tag{1}$$

For the given sequence of words W, and its corresponding label sequence L, joint probability $P(W|L)P(L)$ has to be maximized by the objective function of a generative model.

Recently, Conditional Random Field (Lafferty et al., 2001), a discriminative model has become the popular technique for solving de-identification task (Yang and Garibaldi, 2015). Here, given the word sequence $W_1^N = w_1, ...w_N$, as input, CRF calculates the conditional probability of labels $L_1^N = l_1, ...l_N$, as follows:

$$P(l_1, l_2, ..., l_N | W) = \frac{1}{Z_w} \prod_i (\Psi_i(L_i, W) \Psi_i'(L_i, L_{i-1}, W)) \tag{2}$$

where Ψ_i and Ψ_i' are defined as follows:

$$\Psi_i(L_i, W) = exp(\sum_k \eta_k s_k(l_i, w, i)) \tag{3}$$

$$\Psi_i'(L_i, L_{i-1}, W) = exp(\sum_j \lambda_j t_j(l_i, l_{i-1}, w, i)) \tag{4}$$

where t_j and s_k are transition feature function and state feature function, respectively. The transition feature function t_j depends upon the current label l_i, previous label l_{i-1} and the observation sequence of word w at time i. The state feature function is the function of current label l_i and the observation word w at time i. Parameters λ_j and η_k are to be estimated from training data.

Other variants of discriminative models include Support Vector Machines (SVMs) (Cortes and Vapnik, 1995), where local probability functions are used. With these traditional methodologies, classification algorithm is a black box implementation of linear and log-linear approaches which require good feature engineering. After conducting thorough literature survey, deep learning architecture is found to be one of the successful techniques where both classification and feature designing are done during the learning phase automatically without using any human intervention. Therefore, we propose a technique based on deep learning architecture of RNN. We discuss below the RNN architecture with respect to our chosen problems.

3 Proposed Approach for Patient Data De-identification

The RNN models used for de-identification task are described here.

3.1 Word Embedding

A real-valued representation of a word is the input for our RNN architecture. Word embedding provides an unique property to capture semantics and syntactic information of different words (Mikolov et al., 2013). The underlying idea is that similar words appear in close vicinity of each other. The vector corresponding to each input word w_i is produced whose dimensionality is set at the time of learning the neural language model from the given unsupervised corpus. This representation provides the continuous-space representation for each word. Usually, training of the word embedding is done in an unsupervised manner using external natural language text like Wikipedia, news article, bio-medical literature etc. The architecture can be varied by adopting various architectures like shallow neural networks (Schwenk and Gauvain, 2005), RNN (Mikolov et al., 2010; Mikolov et al., 2011), SENNA (Collobert et al., 2011),

34

word2vec (Mikolov et al., 2013) etc. We use three different procedures to learn word embeddings like random number initialization, RNN's word embedding and continuous bag-of-words (CBOW). For random word embedding we initialize the vector of dimension 100 in the range -0.25 to $+0.25$. In order to evaluate the impact of RNN we use the word embedding as provided by RNNLM [4] of dimension 80 which is trained on Broadcast news corpus. In addition to this we also use word embedding model trained by CBOW technique as proposed in (Mikolov et al., 2013) on news data of dimension 300.

3.2 Word Dependencies captured using a Context Window

In feed forward neural network model we provide input as word embedding of the target word. But, it can not capture the dependency associated with the current word of interest. Context words can capture the short-term temporal dependencies in this setting. Let us assume that each word is being represented by its word embedding vector of length d, the word-context window is the ordered concatenation of word embedding vectors. For word embedding of dimension d and context word of size m, the word vector is constructed as the ordered concatenation of $2m + 1$ word embedding vectors, i.e. m previous words, current word and m next words with the following formula

$$C_m(x_{i-m}^{i+m}) = v_{i-m} \oplus \ldots v_i \ldots \oplus v_{i+m} \tag{5}$$

where $\oplus$ is a concatenation operator. v_i is the word embedding vector of the word x_i.
$x_{i-m}^{i+m} = [x_{i-m} \ldots, x_i, \ldots x_{i+m}]$ represents the concatenation of dependent words in the window size m. In order to generate m context window for the beginning and ending words, padding is performed. We provide an example below to show the generation of context window of size 1 around the word 'suffers':

$$C(t) = [\text{Doe } \textit{suffers } \text{from}] \tag{6}$$

$$C(t) \rightarrow x(t) = [v_{\text{Doe}} \; v_{\textit{suffers}} \; v_{\text{from}}]$$

In this example, $C(t)$ is a 1 word context window. $v_{\textit{suffers}}$ is the embedding vector of word 'suffers' and d is the dimension of the embedding vector. Similarly, $C(t)$ forms the ordered concatenation of word embedding vector for the word sequence $x(t)$ at time t.

3.3 Variants of RNN Architecture: Elman and Jordan

In this section, we discuss two different variants of RNN architecture, Elman (Elman, 1990) and the Jordan models (Jordan, 1997). Figure-1 depicts an architecture for both the models. Feed forward neural network (NN) (Svozil et al., 1997) is the basic biologically inspired neural network model. In variation to feed forward architecture, both the RNN models make connection also with the previous layer. In Elman architecture each state keeps track of its previous hidden layer states by its recurrent connections. Therefore, the hidden layer $h(t)$ at time instance t keeps track of the previous $(t-1)^{th}$ hidden layer i.e., the output of $(t-1)^{th}$ hidden layer is given as the input to the tth hidden layer $h(t)$ along with the context window input $C_m(x_{t-m}^{t+m})$. Mathematically, for H hidden layer, Elman architecture is described as shown below:

$$h^{(1)}(t) = f(W^{(1)}C_m(x_{t-m}^{t+m}) + V^{(1)}h^{(1)}(t-1) + b) \tag{7}$$

$$h^{(H)}(t) = f(W^{(H)}h^{(H-1)}(t) + V^{(H)}h^{(H)}(t-1) + b) \tag{8}$$

In our experiment we have used a non-linear sigmoid function as the activation unit of hidden layer.

$$f(x) = 1/(1 + e^{-x}) \tag{9}$$

The superscript represents the hidden layer depth and, W and V denote the weight connections from input layer to the hidden layer and hidden layer of last state to current hidden layer, respectively. Here, b is a bias term. The softmax function is later applied to the hidden states to generate the posterior probabilities of the classifier for different classes as given below:

$$P(y(t) = i|C_m(x_{t-m}^{t+m})) = g(Uh^{(H)}(t) + c) \tag{10}$$

---

[4]http://rnnlm.org/

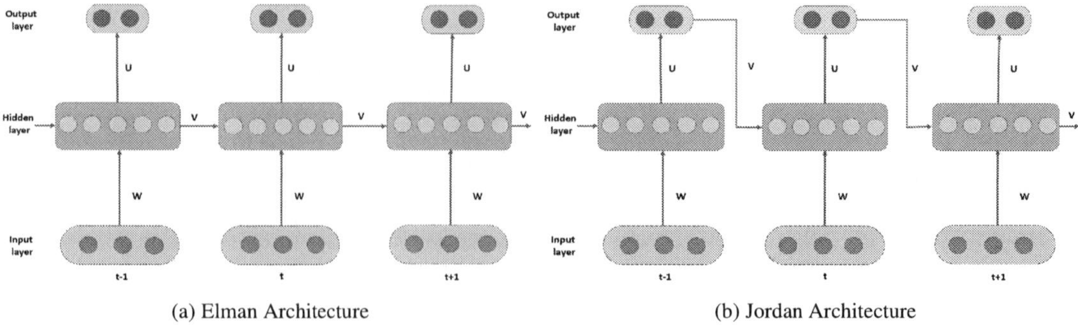

(a) Elman Architecture   (b) Jordan Architecture

Figure 1: RNN architectures of both the variants

Here, U is weight connection from hidden to output layer, c is a bias term and g is softmax function defined as follows:

$$g(z_m) = \frac{e^{z_m}}{\sum_{i=1}^{i=k} e^{z_k}} \tag{11}$$

Jordan model is the another variation of RNN architecture which is similar to the Elman model except the input to the recurrent connections are through the output posterior probabilities:

$$h(t) = f(WC_m(x_{t-m}^{t+m}) + VP(y(t-1)) + b) \tag{12}$$

where W and V denote the weight connection between input to hidden layer and output layer of previous state to current hidden layer and $P(y(t-1))$ is the posterior probability of last word of interest. The sigmoid function described in Eq-9 is used as non-linear activation function f.

3.4 Datasets

The dataset used to evaluate our proposed architecture is obtained from 2014 I2b2 challenge (Stubbs et al., 2015). This dataset is obtained from "Research Patient Data Repository of Partners Healthcare". A total of 1304 medical records were manually annotated. In order to use this data for our experiment we split the data set into three parts: training, validation and test. The detailed distribution of different PHI terms in these three sets are described in Table-2.

Our training data compromises of 11,911 PHI relevant instances, while the test dataset consists of total 1253 PHI instances which we developed from I2B2-2014 training data. To ensure the patient confidentiality as much as possible, the challenge aims to identify HIPAA-PHI categories firstly with the added subcategories. This dataset is annotated using seven main PHI categories with the twenty-five associated subcategories. While, our experiments cover the seven main PHI categories, I2b2 challenge covers almost all HIPAA defined categories and subcategories. The list of categories as well as subcategories are 1. Name (subtypes: Patient, Doctor, Username), 2. Profession, 3. Location (subtypes: Hospital, Department, Organization, Room, Street, City, State, Country, ZIP), 4. Age, 5. Date, 6. Contact (subtypes: Phone, Fax, Email, URL, IPAddress), 7. Ids (subtypes: Medical Record Number, Health Plan Number, Social Security Number, Account Number, Vehicle ID, Device ID, Licence Number, Biometric ID). In this work, the aim is to identify seven different PHI subtypes; *Patient, Doctor, Hospital, Location, Phone, ID* and *Date* from the above defined categories. In order to evaluate the model performance well known evaluation metrics such as recall, precision and F-Measure are used.

3.5 RNN Hyper-Parameters and Learning

The RNN hyper-parameters are number of hidden units (H), learning rate (λ), context window size (m), no. of epochs (e^n) and dropout probability (p). In order to find optimal hyper-parameter values we experiment with different parameter settings. The optimal hyper-parameter values for both the RNN architectures are listed in Table-3. The embedding matrix and the weight matrices are initialized from

36

PHI category	Train	Validation	Test
DOCTOR	2262	183	236
HOSPITAL	1342	141	164
DATE	4154	377	498
PATIENT	707	28	59
LOCATION	93	14	19
PHONE	153	12	13
ID	3200	233	264
Total	**11911**	**988**	**1253**

Table 2: Data set statistics: distribution of different classes for training, test and validation sets.

Parameter's	E-RNN	J-RNN
Hidden layer size	100	150
learning rate	0.01	0.01
Dropout probability	0.5	0.5
no. of epochs	25	25
context window size	11	9

Table 3: Optimal values of hyper-parameters for different RNN architectures

the uniform distribution in the range [-1,1]. In order to train RNN we use stochastic gradient descent. We consider the whole sentence as a mini-batch and perform one update per sentence, towards minimizing the negative log-likelihood.

3.6 Regularization

In order to prevent network from over-fitting we use dropout technique (Hinton et al., 2012). Dropout omits the portion of hidden unit from each training sample before passing it to the final softmax layer. We set dropout probability p as 0.5 throughout the experiments in both the variations of RNN.

3.7 Impact of Word Embedding Techniques

Table-4 shows the impact of each word embedding techniques with Elman architecture. The word vectors obtained from the RNNLM performed well on syntactic part. It is obvious because the word vectors in the RNNLM are directly connected to a non-linear hidden layer. The CBOW architecture works better than RNNLM for the syntactic tasks, and about the same on the semantic tasks. The CBOW model follows the distributional hypothesis while training which enables to outperform over the other word embedding techniques.

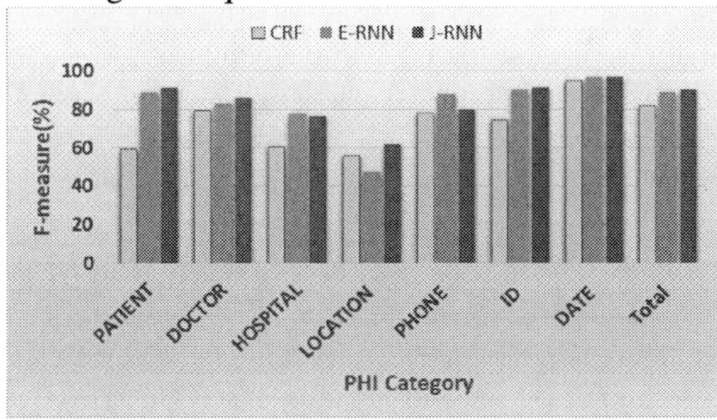

Figure 2: Performance comparisons between RNN and CRF for all identified PHI types

Word Embedding Techniques	dimension (d)	Precision	Recall	F-Measure
Random Number	100	87.19	85.48	86.32
RNNLM	80	88.21	87.32	87.76
CBOW	300	89.35	89.55	89.44

Table 4: Impact of fine-tuned word embedding technique using Elman architecture. Here RNNLM: Word embedding obtained from the RNN language modeling technique(Mikolov et al., 2010). CBOW: The CBoW takes the context word as input and tries to predict the target word.

3.8 Results with Lexical Features

In the literature there are quite a few works of patient data de-identification using lexical features such as PoS, character n-gram, chunk information etc. In the literature, it has been shown that CRF is a robust classifier for this task. In addition to the RNN we also perform experiments with some useful hand-crafted features by considering CRF as the base classifier. The hand-crafted features that we use for CRF are as follows:

1. Context word feature: We use current word and the words within the context window of length 3 as features.

PHI	CRF Baseline			E-RNN			J-RNN		
category	R	P	F	R	P	F	R	P	F
PATIENT NAME	60.87	57.14	58.95	86.96	90.91	88.89	91.30	91.30	91.30
DOCTOR NAME	80.43	77.78	79.08	82.55	83.98	83.26	85.11	86.58	85.84
HOSPITAL NAME	47.24	83.70	60.39	73.01	83.80	78.03	70.55	83.33	76.41
LOCATION	52.63	58.82	55.56	57.89	40.74	47.83	68.42	56.52	61.90
PHONE	69.23	90.00	78.26	84.62	91.67	88.00	76.92	83.33	80.00
ID	75.86	73.06	74.44	89.27	91.37	90.31	90.80	92.58	91.68
DATE	95.17	94.22	94.69	98.39	95.14	96.74	98.39	95.32	96.83
Overall	**79.74**	**83.11**	**81.39**	**88.90**	**89.55**	**89.22**	**89.63**	**90.73**	**90.18**

Table 5: Detailed performance analysis with different models for PHI identification task. Here **R,P** and **F** denotes *Recall, Precision* and *F-score* respectively.

2. Bag-of-word feature: This feature includes uni-grams, bi-grams, tri-grams of the target token. We use window size of [-2, 2] with respect to the target token. Here, n-gram is referred as the continuous sequence of n items. An n-gram generated having sizes of $1, 2, 3$ are known as an uni-gram, bi-gram and tri-gram, respectively.

3. Part-of-Speech (PoS) Information: The PoS information of current word, previous two words and the next two words are used as features. We obtain PoS of words from the Stanford tagger (Toutanova and Manning, 2000).

4. Chunk Information: The chunk information is an important feature to identify the PHI term-boundary. We use chunk information obtained from *openNLP*[5].

5. Combined POS-token and Chunk-token Feature: This feature is generated by the combination of other token features like PoS, Chunk within the context window of [-1, 1]. This is represented as $[w_0p_{-1}, w_0p_0, w_0p_1]$ where w_0 represents the target word, and p_{-1}, p_0 and p_1 represent the previous, current and the next POS or Chunk tags, respectively.

We build our model by incorporating the above features. We use the CRF implementation[6] of CRF^{++} with default parameter settings. Detailed results on PHI identification task using these features with CRF classifier are shown in Table-5.

3.9   Results with RNN

The Elman architecture that we discussed in Subsection-3.3 has been applied to identify the PHI terms from medical records. Table-5 shows the detailed results of E-RNN on individual PHI categories as well as the overall results. The E-RNN performs better than our CRF baseline model. The experiments are performed with all the types of word embedding techniques discussed in Subsection-3.7. The CBoW based word embedding, when given as input to E-RNN model, performs well over the other word embedding based techniques as shown in Table 4. Experimental results on Jordan architecture are shown in Table-5. The performance that we obtain shows better performance over the baseline. We show detailed comparative results in Table-5. Experiments reveal that J-RNN model performs superior compared E-RNN in identifying 5 PHI categories out of total 7.

4   Error Analysis

We perform detailed error analysis on outputs produced in both the models. We divide the major sources of errors in three different categories. Following observations can be made:

---

[5]https://opennlp.apache.org/
[6]https://taku910.github.io/crfpp/

- MISSED ENTITY: This error occurs when the entity is present in the gold-standard data, but the system fails to identify it as an entity. We calculate a total of 106 and 95 cases in Elman and Jordan model, respectively, for such cases. The possible causes are:

  - Presence of single-word person name: These words are difficult to detect as compared with full names (consist of more than one words) due to the lack of context and morphology. These errors are more dominated in case of 'Doctor' and 'Patient' categories.

  - Presence of abbreviated words: These errors are dominated mostly in case of 'Hospital' and 'Doctor' categories as the system lacks in identifying the short words (e.g., "FIH", "WA") due to the presence of ambiguous non-PHI terms.

  - Presence of unseen terms: The words not seen during training contribute to this error. These cases are mostly found for 'Location', and 'Hospital' categories.

- WRONG ENTITY: This error is obtained when the entity obtained is correct but belongs to some other type. In total 223 and 164 instances are mis-classified in case of Elman and Jordan model, respectively. The major causes of actual errors are as follows:

  - Inter-PHI ambiguity: These errors are obtained mostly in case of 'Doctor' and 'Patient' categories. As the name-forms are quite similar to each other, these PHI terms are highly ambiguous. This error arises most of the times when the names consist of single words. For example "Glass", "Chabechird" etc. These cases are also observed in case of 'Location' category.

- FALSE POSITIVES: This error occurs when the system lacks in identifying the proper boundary of the entity. Either the entity has additional part or the missing part. These errors are mostly seen in case of 'Doctor' and 'Hospital' categories. The major cause of this error is:

  - Presence of long compounded words: If the entity consists of more than 3 words, the system fails to identify those correctly. For example "Tawn List Medical Center".

4.1 Discussions

Two different RNN architectures, E-RNN and J-RNN, perform well over the baseline model based on machine learning technique. The J-RNN outperforms the E-RNN model in most of the PHI category detection. The J-RNN model takes the outputs of previous iteration along with the outputs of current hidden layer to classify the current word. It would be the possible reason behind the better system performance for strict[7] PHI (Patient, Doctor) as compared to the performance of E-RNN for the same. It should be noted that due to computational limitation, we were not able to use whole dataset as such we were unable to make any direct comparison with the existing systems. Most of the existing systems are supervised in nature and makes use of hand-crafted feature set and rules. These techniques require much feature engineering. The development of quality features are challenging and time-consuming. In our case, we don't use any hand-crafted feature set, but still achieves good performance level.

5 Conclusions and Future Works

In this paper we present a deep neural network based approach for patient data de-identification. This has been designed to identify and classify Protected Health Information (PHI) present in free-text medical records and encrypt these for preserving the privacy of patients. We systematically implement and compare different variants of RNN architecture, including Elman and Jordan. In order to compare we also develop a CRF based model with the traditional features. We observe that both the variants of RNN architecture outperform the baseline built using popular CRF based model. We have observed the performance improvement of 7.83% with Elman and 8.79% with Jordan over the baseline model. In future, we would like to explore more advanced deep learning techniques like Long Short term Memory (LSTM) using the full dataset and on other domains as well.

---

[7]Since it is a kind of multiword NE's, in which previous label information is vital to identify the current

Acknowledgements

Authors gratefully acknowledge for the partial support received from "Sushrut: ezDI Research Lab on Health Informatics", Department of Computer Science and Engineering, IIT Patna, India.

References

Dzmitry Bahdanau, Kyunghyun Cho, and Yoshua Bengio. 2014. Neural machine translation by jointly learning to align and translate. *arXiv preprint arXiv:1409.0473*.

Tim Beck, Sirisha Gollapudi, Søren Brunak, Norbert Graf, Heinz U Lemke, Debasis Dash, Iain Buchan, Carlos Díaz, Ferran Sanz, and Anthony J Brookes. 2012. Knowledge engineering for health: a new discipline required to bridge the ict gap between research and healthcare. *Human mutation*, 33(5):797–802.

Ronan Collobert, Jason Weston, Léon Bottou, Michael Karlen, Koray Kavukcuoglu, and Pavel Kuksa. 2011. Natural language processing (almost) from scratch. *Journal of Machine Learning Research*, 12(Aug):2493–2537.

Corinna Cortes and Vladimir Vapnik. 1995. Support-vector networks. *Machine learning*, 20(3):273–297.

Jeffrey L Elman. 1990. Finding structure in time. *Cognitive science*, 14(2):179–211.

Yikun Guo, Robert Gaizauskas, Ian Roberts, George Demetriou, and Mark Hepple. 2006. Identifying personal health information using support vector machines. In *i2b2 workshop on challenges in natural language processing for clinical data*, pages 10–11. Citeseer.

Kazuo Hara. 2006. Applying a svm based chunker and a text classifier to the deid challenge. In *i2b2 Workshop on challenges in natural language processing for clinical data*, pages 10–11. Am Med Inform Assoc.

Bin He, Yi Guan, Jianyi Cheng, Keting Cen, and Wenlan Hua. 2015. Crfs based de-identification of medical records. *Journal of biomedical informatics*, 58:S39–S46.

Geoffrey E Hinton, Nitish Srivastava, Alex Krizhevsky, Ilya Sutskever, and Ruslan R Salakhutdinov. 2012. Improving neural networks by preventing co-adaptation of feature detectors. *arXiv preprint arXiv:1207.0580*.

Michael I Jordan. 1997. Serial order: A parallel distributed processing approach. *Advances in psychology*, 121:471–495.

Yoon Kim. 2014. Convolutional neural networks for sentence classification. *arXiv preprint arXiv:1408.5882*.

John Lafferty, Andrew McCallum, and Fernando Pereira. 2001. Conditional random fields: Probabilistic models for segmenting and labeling sequence data. In *Proceedings of the eighteenth international conference on machine learning, ICML*, volume 1, pages 282–289.

Grégoire Mesnil, Xiaodong He, Li Deng, and Yoshua Bengio. 2013. Investigation of recurrent-neural-network architectures and learning methods for spoken language understanding. In *INTERSPEECH*, pages 3771–3775.

Stéphane M Meystre, Guergana K Savova, Karin C Kipper-Schuler, John F Hurdle, et al. 2008. Extracting information from textual documents in the electronic health record: a review of recent research. *Yearb Med Inform*, 35:128–44.

Tomas Mikolov, Martin Karafiát, Lukas Burget, Jan Cernocký, and Sanjeev Khudanpur. 2010. Recurrent neural network based language model. In *Interspeech*, volume 2, page 3.

Tomáš Mikolov, Stefan Kombrink, Lukáš Burget, Jan Černocký, and Sanjeev Khudanpur. 2011. Extensions of recurrent neural network language model. In *2011 IEEE International Conference on Acoustics, Speech and Signal Processing (ICASSP)*, pages 5528–5531. IEEE.

Tomas Mikolov, Kai Chen, Greg Corrado, and Jeffrey Dean. 2013. Efficient estimation of word representations in vector space. *arXiv preprint arXiv:1301.3781*.

Holger Schwenk and Jean-Luc Gauvain. 2005. Training neural network language models on very large corpora. In *Proceedings of the conference on Human Language Technology and Empirical Methods in Natural Language Processing*, pages 201–208. Association for Computational Linguistics.

Richard Socher, Alex Perelygin, Jean Y Wu, Jason Chuang, Christopher D Manning, Andrew Y Ng, and Christopher Potts. 2013. Recursive deep models for semantic compositionality over a sentiment treebank. In *Proceedings of the conference on empirical methods in natural language processing (EMNLP)*, volume 1631, page 1642. Citeseer.

Amber Stubbs, Christopher Kotfila, and Özlem Uzuner. 2015. Automated systems for the de-identification of longitudinal clinical narratives: Overview of 2014 i2b2/uthealth shared task track 1. *Journal of biomedical informatics*, 58:S11–S19.

Daniel Svozil, Vladimir Kvasnicka, and Jiri Pospichal. 1997. Introduction to multi-layer feed-forward neural networks. *Chemometrics and intelligent laboratory systems*, 39(1):43–62.

György Szarvas, Richárd Farkas, and András Kocsor. 2006. A multilingual named entity recognition system using boosting and c4. 5 decision tree learning algorithms. In *International Conference on Discovery Science*, pages 267–278. Springer.

Kristina Toutanova and Christopher D Manning. 2000. Enriching the knowledge sources used in a maximum entropy part-of-speech tagger. In *Proceedings of the 2000 Joint SIGDAT conference on Empirical methods in natural language processing and very large corpora: held in conjunction with the 38th Annual Meeting of the Association for Computational Linguistics-Volume 13*, pages 63–70. Association for Computational Linguistics.

Jason Weston, Antoine Bordes, Sumit Chopra, Alexander M Rush, Bart van Merriënboer, Armand Joulin, and Tomas Mikolov. 2015. Towards ai-complete question answering: A set of prerequisite toy tasks. *arXiv preprint arXiv:1502.05698*.

Hui Yang and Jonathan M Garibaldi. 2015. Automatic detection of protected health information from clinic narratives. *Journal of biomedical informatics*, 58:S30–S38.

Neural Clinical Paraphrase Generation with Attention

Sadid A. Hasan[1], Bo Liu[2], Joey Liu[1], Ashequl Qadir[1],
Kathy Lee[1], Vivek Datla[1], Aaditya Prakash[1,3], Oladimeji Farri[1]

[1]Artificial Intelligence Laboratory, Philips Research North America, Cambridge, MA, USA
[2]Auburn University, Auburn, AL, USA
[3]Brandeis University, Waltham, MA, USA

`{sadid.hasan,joey.liu}@philips.com, {boliu}@auburn.edu`
`{ashequl.qadir,kathy.lee_1,vivek.datla,dimeji.farri}@philips.com`
`{aaditya.prakash,aprakash}@{philips.com,brandeis.edu}`

Abstract

Paraphrase generation is important in various applications such as search, summarization, and question answering due to its ability to generate textual alternatives while keeping the overall meaning intact. Clinical paraphrase generation is especially vital in building patient-centric clinical decision support (CDS) applications where users are able to understand complex clinical jargons via easily comprehensible alternative paraphrases. This paper presents *Neural Clinical Paraphrase Generation (NCPG)*, a novel approach that casts the task as a monolingual neural machine translation (NMT) problem. We propose an end-to-end neural network built on an attention-based bidirectional Recurrent Neural Network (RNN) architecture with an encoder-decoder framework to perform the task. Conventional bilingual NMT models mostly rely on word-level modeling and are often limited by out-of-vocabulary (OOV) issues. In contrast, we represent the source and target paraphrase pairs as character sequences to address this limitation. To the best of our knowledge, this is the first work that uses attention-based RNNs for clinical paraphrase generation and also proposes an end-to-end character-level modeling for this task. Extensive experiments on a large curated clinical paraphrase corpus show that the attention-based NCPG models achieve improvements of up to 5.2 BLEU points and 0.5 METEOR points over a non-attention based strong baseline for word-level modeling, whereas further gains of up to 6.1 BLEU points and 1.3 METEOR points are obtained by the character-level NCPG models over their word-level counterparts. Overall, our models demonstrate comparable performance relative to the state-of-the-art phrase-based non-neural models.

1 Introduction

Paraphrasing, the act of generating the same semantic content as the source in the same language, can help gain performance improvements in many NLP applications. Examples include generating query variants or pattern alternatives for information retrieval, information extraction or question answering systems, creating reference paraphrases for automatic evaluation of machine translation and document summarization systems, and generating concise or simplified information for sentence compression or sentence simplification systems (Madnani and Dorr, 2010; Androutsopoulos and Malakasiotis, 2010). In particular, paraphrase generation has a significant value in developing patient-centric intelligent clinical decision support (CDS) applications where users are able to understand complex clinical jargons via easily comprehensible alternative paraphrases (Elhadad and Sutaria, 2007; Deléger and Zweigenbaum, 2009). For example, the complex clinical term *"nocturnal enuresis"* can be paraphrased as *"nocturnal incontinence of urine"* or *"bedwetting"* to better clarify a well-known condition associated with children.

Traditional paraphrase generation methods exploit hand-crafted rules (McKeown, 1983) or automatically learned complex paraphrase patterns (Zhao et al., 2009), use thesaurus-based (Hassan et al., 2007) or semantic analysis driven natural language generation approaches (Kozlowski et al., 2003), or leverage statistical machine learning theory and principles (Quirk et al., 2004; Wubben et al., 2010). In contrast, inspired by the recent success of bilingual neural machine translation (NMT) (Kalchbrenner and

42

Proceedings of the Clinical Natural Language Processing Workshop,
pages 42–53, Osaka, Japan, December 11-17 2016.
"

Blunsom, 2013; Sutskever et al., 2014; Cho et al., 2014b; Bahdanau et al., 2015) that shows promising performance compared to the traditional statistical machine translation (SMT) approaches, we propose neural clinical paraphrase generation (NCPG) by casting the task as a monolingual NMT problem. Unlike bilingual machine translation, monolingual machine translation considers the source language the same as the target language, which allows for its adaptation as a paraphrase generation task.

SMT systems (Koehn et al., 2003; Koehn, 2010) use a noisy channel model to identify an optimal target sentence that maximizes its conditional probability given a source sentence. Ideally, this process uses the Bayes' rule to distinctly maximize the KL-divergence between a language model and a translation model from a monolingual and a parallel corpus, respectively. However, NMT models are built from training a single end-to-end neural network architecture on a large parallel corpus that can directly optimize the conditional probability of an underlying sentence pair. Such models typically follow an encoder-decoder approach by building a pair of neural networks, where the first network acts as an encoder to generate a fixed-length vector representation of the source sentence, which is in turn decoded by the second network to form a target sentence (Sutskever et al., 2014; Cho et al., 2014b). Recurrent Neural Network (RNN) architectures with Long Short-Term Memory (LSTM) (Hochreiter and Schmidhuber, 1997) or Gated Recurrent Units (GRU) (Cho et al., 2014a) are generally utilized to train the end-to-end state-of-the-art NMT systems. Another effective NMT model has been proposed recently, which follows an attention-based soft-search approach to improve the performance of the encoder-decoder architectures (Bahdanau et al., 2015). We use an attention-based bidirectional RNN architecture (Schuster and Paliwal, 1997; Bahdanau et al., 2015) with an encoder-decoder framework to build our NCPG models. Bidirectional RNNs have been shown to outperform unidirectional RNNs for sequence to sequence learning tasks (Jean et al., 2015).

NMT models mostly rely on word-level modeling that often causes an out-of-vocabulary (OOV) issue while predicting a target word given an unknown source word (Luong et al., 2015b). To address this limitation, we represent the source and target paraphrase pairs as character sequences and propose a character-level encoder-decoder framework for clinical paraphrase generation. To the best of our knowledge, this work is the first to adapt monolingual NMT for clinical paraphrase generation using an attention-based mechanism and also propose an end-to-end character-level NCPG model.

Extensive experiments on a large curated clinical paraphrase corpus built on a benchmark parallel paraphrase database, PPDB 2.0 (Pavlick et al., 2015b), along with a comprehensive medical metathesaurus (Lindberg et al., 1993) show that the proposed attention-based NCPG model can outperform an RNN encoder-decoder based strong baseline for word-level modeling, whereas character-level models can achieve further improvements over their word-level counterparts. Overall, the proposed models demonstrate comparable performance relative to the state-of-the-art phrase-based conventional machine translation models. The main contributions of our paper can be summarized as follows:

- We presented a novel approach for clinical paraphrase generation by casting the task as a monolingual neural machine translation problem. We proposed an end-to-end neural network model built on an attention-based bidirectional Recurrent Neural Network (RNN) architecture (Bahdanau et al., 2015) with an encoder-decoder framework to perform the task.

- We also presented a novel character-based neural clinical paraphrase generation approach to overcome the OOV issues encountered by the word-level models.

- We built a large curated paraphrase corpus using a benchmark parallel paraphrase database, PPDB 2.0 (Pavlick et al., 2015b) along with a comprehensive medical metathesaurus, UMLS (Lindberg et al., 1993) for our experiments.

- We conducted rigorous automatic and manual evaluations of our models. Results demonstrated that our proposed attention-based NCPG model can outperform an RNN encoder-decoder based strong baseline for word-level modeling, whereas character-level models can achieve further improvements. Overall, our models showed comparable performance relative to the state-of-the-art phrase-based non-neural machine translation models.

2   Related Work

Deep learning has been successfully applied to various NLP tasks in recent years. There are works that effectively apply recursive autoencoders (Socher et al., 2011) and convolutional neural networks (Yin and Schütze, 2015) for paraphrase recognition. However, paraphrase generation is a harder task due to the requirement of constructing semantically similar, grammatically accurate alternatives to a source sentence, and no prior work has attempted to solve this problem using deep learning.

Prior work that regards paraphrase generation as a monolingual machine translation task typically uses (non-neural) statistical machine translation (SMT) principles. Quirk et al. (2004) show the effectiveness of SMT techniques for paraphrase generation given adequate monolingual parallel corpus extracted from comparable news articles. Wubben et al. (2010) propose a phrase-based SMT framework for sentential paraphrase generation by using a large aligned monolingual corpus of news headlines. Zhao et al. (2008) propose a combination of multiple resources to learn phrase-based paraphrase tables and corresponding feature functions to devise a log-linear SMT model. Other models generate application-specific paraphrases (Zhao et al., 2009), leverage bilingual parallel corpora (Bannard and Callison-Burch, 2005) or apply a multi-pivot approach to output candidate paraphrases (Zhao et al., 2010).

Recently proposed NMT systems have shown excellent performance compared to the SMT systems by using RNN-based end-to-end deep neural network architectures (Sutskever et al., 2014; Cho et al., 2014b). Previous works that deploy RNNs have shown favorable results to model variable-length sequential inputs (Schuster and Paliwal, 1997; Sutskever et al., 2011; Graves, 2013; Kalchbrenner and Blunsom, 2013; Sperduti, 2015) while attention-based NMT models have shown better performance than the traditional encoder-decoder frameworks (Bahdanau et al., 2015; Luong et al., 2015a).

State-of-the-art NMT models usually perform word-level computations by limiting the size of the source and the target vocabulary and hence, suffer from OOV issues due to vocabulary incompatibility. This phenomenon may arise when a trained model has to deal with a previously unseen word during the testing phase (Luong et al., 2015b). Jean et al. (2015) use a large target vocabulary to address OOV issues for word-level NMT models while Luong et al. (2015b) introduce a post-processing step to translate OOV words using a dictionary. Since these approaches depend heavily on the time- and cost-effective process of developing or acquiring large volume dictionaries that may not scale across several domains, OOV issues still limit the accuracy of the word-based models. Based on the recent success of character-level modeling in resolving the OOV limitation (Bojanowski et al., 2015; Kim et al., 2015; Ling et al., 2015; Costa-Jussà and Fonollosa, 2016; Chung et al., 2016), we propose a character-level NCPG model and perform relative comparisons with the word-level models.

Depending on the level of granularity, there can be different types of paraphrasing such as: lexical (e.g. *<automobile, car>*), phrasal (e.g. *<carry on, persist in>*), and sentential (e.g. *<The book was interesting, I enjoyed reading the book>*) (Madnani and Dorr, 2010). Earlier work related to clinical-domain specific paraphrasing uses some unsupervised textual similarity measures to generate/extract lexical and phrasal paraphrases from monolingual parallel and comparable corpora (Elhadad and Sutaria, 2007; Deléger and Zweigenbaum, 2009). Prud'hommeaux and Roark (2015) propose a graph-based word alignment algorithm to examine neurological disorders through analysis of spoken language data. Another loosely related recent work adopts a semi-supervised word embedding model for medical synonym extraction (Wang et al., 2015) that can be regarded as the simplest form of a lexical paraphrase extraction task. Our work is the first to propose a neural network-based architecture that can model word/character sequences to essentially address all granularities of paraphrase generation for the clinical domain.

For our experiments, we combine the *Paraphrase Database (PPDB) 2.0* (Pavlick et al., 2015b) with a large medical metathesaurus, known as *Unified Medical Language System (UMLS)* (Lindberg et al., 1993) to build a comprehensive monolingual parallel paraphrase corpus such that the proposed NCPG models can effectively learn discriminatory features related to complex clinical terms. Similar methods of combining general and domain-specific data have been proven to be useful for domain-focused paraphrasing tasks in the literature (Pavlick et al., 2015a).

3 Model Description

3.1 Task Formulation

Our NCPG system is an attention-based bidirectional RNN architecture (Schuster and Paliwal, 1997) that uses an encoder-decoder framework (Bahdanau et al., 2015). We construct different NCPG models by representing the source and target paraphrase pairs as word or character-level sequences.

The neural clinical paraphrase generation task can be formulated as follows: given a source sequence $x = x_0, \ldots, x_L$, generate a target paraphrase sequence $y = y_0, \ldots, y_M$, where x_i ($0 \leq i \leq L$) and y_j ($0 \leq j \leq M$) are the individual textual units (word/character), and L, M are the respective lengths of the source and the target sequences. Ideally, generation of the next target unit y_n depends on the source sequence x and the already generated target units $y_0, \ldots, y_{n-1}$. In the following subsections, we present a description of the generic RNN architecture and the attention-based NCPG model.

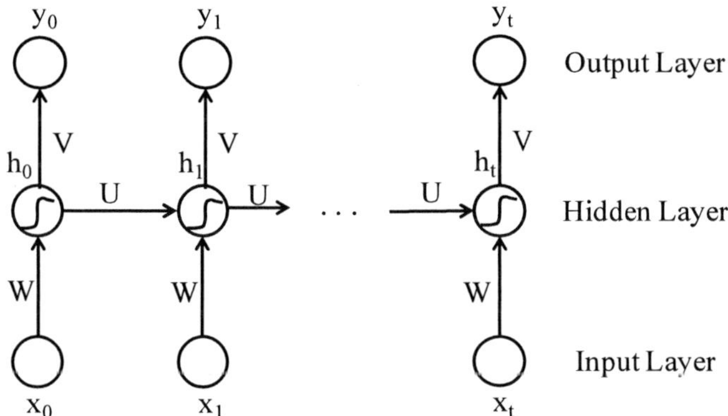

Figure 1: Generic recurrent neural network architecture.

3.2 Recurrent Neural Network (RNN)

RNNs are particularly suitable for modeling sequences and have been shown to perform well to solve various NLP tasks because of their ability to deal with variable-length input and output (Sutskever et al., 2011). The RNN network architecture is similar to the standard feedforward neural network with the exception that hidden unit activation at a particular time t is dependent on that of time $t - 1$.

Figure 1 shows an unrolled RNN architecture, where x_t, y_t, h_t are the input, output, and hidden state at time step t, and W, U, V are the parameters of the model corresponding to *input*, *hidden*, and *output* layer weights (shared across all time steps).

The hidden state h_t is essentially the memory of the network as it can capture necessary information about an input sequence by exploiting the previous hidden state h_{t-1} and the current input x_t as follows:

$$h_t = f(Wx_t + Uh_{t-1}), \tag{1}$$

where f is an element-wise nonlinear activation function. The output y_t is computed similarly as a function of the memory at time t: Vh_t. Although RNN is theoretically a powerful model to encode sequential information, in practice it often suffers from the vanishing/exploding gradient problems while learning long-range dependencies (Bengio et al., 1994). LSTM (Hochreiter and Schmidhuber, 1997) and GRU (Cho et al., 2014a) networks are known to be successful remedies to these problems. We use GRU as the hidden layer activation unit in our paraphrase generation framework.

GRU is a simplified version of LSTM with less number of parameters per unit, thus the total number of parameters can be greatly reduced for a large neural network (Cho et al., 2014a). In contrast to LSTM, GRU does not have an internal memory state and the output gate, rather it introduces two gates termed *update* and *reset* as alternatives to the LSTM components. Specifically, GRU computes the hidden state h_t as follows:

$$z_t = \sigma(W^z x_t + U^z h_{t-1})$$
$$r_t = \sigma(W^r x_t + U^r h_{t-1})$$
$$k_t = \tanh(W^k x_t + U^k(r_t \odot h_{t-1}))$$
$$h_t = (1 - z_t) \odot k_t + z_t \odot h_{t-1}, \tag{2}$$

where z_t, r_t are the update gate and the reset gate, and k_t is the candidate hidden state. Note that, z_t, r_t are computed similarly as LSTM (using different weight parameters) where z_t determines how much of the old memory to keep while r_t denotes how much new information is needed to be combined with the old memory. Finally, k_t is computed by exploiting r_t, and h_t is calculated to denote the amount of information needed to be transmitted to the following layers.

3.3 Neural Clinical Paraphrase Generation (NCPG)

The architectural diagram of our paraphrase generation model is presented in Figure 2. In the encoder-decoder framework of our NCPG model, the encoder uses a bidirectional RNN architecture (Schuster and Paliwal, 1997; Bahdanau et al., 2015) where one forward RNN reads the input sequence to generate a hidden state sequence $(\overrightarrow{h_0}, \ldots, \overrightarrow{h_L})$ and one backward RNN reads the input sequence in the reverse order to generate a backward hidden state sequence $(\overleftarrow{h_0}, \ldots, \overleftarrow{h_L})$ using the GRU framework presented in Eq. 2.

Then, an annotation vector h_i for each textual unit x_i is obtained by concatenating the corresponding forward and backward hidden states as follows:

$$h_i = \begin{bmatrix} \overrightarrow{h_i} \\ \overleftarrow{h_i} \end{bmatrix} \tag{3}$$

Thus, h_i encodes all relevant information about the neighboring words or characters of x_i that is used in the decoding phase to compute the context vector of a potential target textual unit.

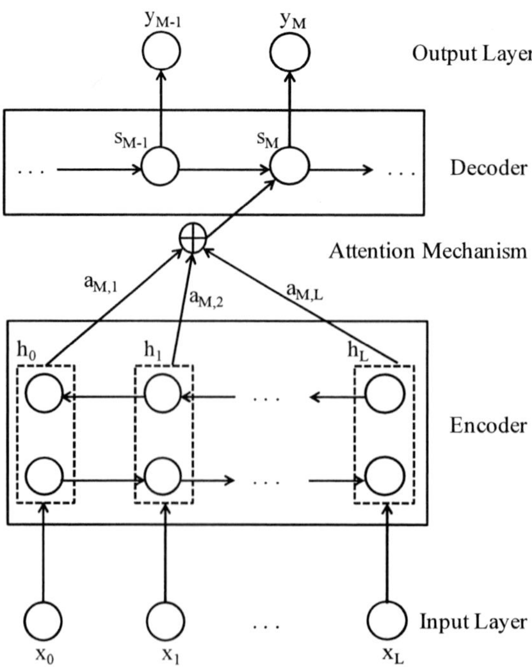

Figure 2: Model architecture for neural clinical paraphrase generation.

The decoder of our model consists of a forward RNN that is built over the generated paraphrase sequence $y = y_0, \ldots, y_{M-1}$ by creating a hidden state sequence $(\overrightarrow{s_0}, \ldots, \overrightarrow{s_{M-1}})$ where s_{M-1} essentially encodes the context of the currently generated paraphrase units. Ideally, at each time step t, an attention mechanism in the decoder computes a relevance score a_{ti} for each annotation vector h_i and sums the weighted annotation vectors as the context vector c_t while generating the next paraphrase word/character y_t. Formally, c_t is computed as follows:

$$c_t = \sum_{i=0}^{L} a_{ti} h_i \tag{4}$$

The annotation relevance score a_{ti} determines the most relevant source unit to focus on and is computed as:

$$a_{ti} = \frac{\exp(e_{ti})}{\sum_{k=0}^{L} \exp(e_{tk})} \tag{5}$$

where e_{ti} is called the *alignment* model that determines how closely the source context at position i matches with the output at position t. e_{ti} is calculated with a feedforward neural network f based on the candidate annotation vector h_i and the previous hidden state s_{t-1} as:

$$e_{ti} = f(s_{t-1}, h_i) \tag{6}$$

Thus, the hidden state s_t of the decoder is computed by the forward RNN based on the previous hidden state s_{t-1}, previously generated textual units y_{t-1}, and the most relevant source context c_t:

$$s_t = g(s_{t-1}, y_{t-1}, c_t) \tag{7}$$

where g is the GRU unit as described in Eq. 2. The conditional distribution over the textual units is computed similarly using a feedforward neural network as follows:

$$P(y_M \mid y_1, \ldots, y_{M-1}, x) = f(y_{M-1}, s_M, c_M) \tag{8}$$

Thus, our encoder-decoder based NCPG model is jointly trained to maximize the conditional log-likelihood of the underlying monolingual parallel paraphrase corpus.

4 Experimental Setup

4.1 Corpus

We combine a publicly available large paraphrase corpus, *Paraphrase Database (PPDB) 2.0* (Pavlick et al., 2015b) with a large clinical database curated from the UMLS metathesaurus (Lindberg et al., 1993) to build a comprehensive monolingual parallel corpus. PPDB leverages multiple bilingual parallel corpora to construct millions of general domain paraphrases in different languages. PPDB 2.0 uses a supervised regression model-based ranking strategy to generate six database categories based on size. In this work, we use the English *S-size* pack[1] database with lexical and phrasal paraphrases.

We extract a subset of 1.2M paraphrases from PPDB with 3.3M words that contain only alphabetic characters. In addition, we consider all unique fully specified terms along with corresponding description terms from SNOMED CT (Cornet and de Keizer, 2008) as source and target paraphrases (total $140K$). The SNOMED CT terms are selected based on UMLS concept unique identifiers (CUI). For example, the fully specified term *"sensorineural hearing loss"* is set as the source and the corresponding description terms such as *"perceptive hearing loss"*, *"perceptive deafness"*, *"sensorineural deafness"*, and *"neurosensory deafness"* are set as the target paraphrases. Three-fifth of the combined corpus is used as the training set while the rest is equally divided into two parts to produce validation and test sets. We use a randomly selected subset of 5000 paraphrases from the test set to evaluate the performance of the proposed models.

We perform normalization with respect to case and standard tokenization to pre-process the dataset. For word-level models, a list of $30K$ most frequent words in each of the source and the target paraphrase set is used for training, while any out-of-vocabulary word is treated as a special *UNK* token. For char-level models, we tokenize text sequences into white-space delimited characters and use a special character (#) to preserve word boundaries.

---

[1] The S-size database pack is used since it contains only the highest scoring paraphrase pairs.

4.2 Models

For comparison, two types of models are trained. The first model (*NCPG-1*) is our baseline, which is built on a non-attention based RNN encoder-decoder framework (Cho et al., 2014b; Cho et al., 2014a; Sutskever et al., 2014), where an encoder (RNN) generates a fixed-length vector representation of the input sequence and a decoder (another RNN) is used to form a output sequence from this representation. The second model (*NCPG-2*) is our proposed attention-based bidirectional RNN encoder-decoder framework. Both models are trained with word-level and character-level sequences (for source-target paraphrase pairs) resulting in four neural clinical paraphrase generation models.

We use a one-hot vector approach to represent the textual units (words/chars) in all models. Each RNN is built with 1000 hidden units (i.e. GRU as discussed in Section 3.2). Models are trained with a stochastic gradient descent (SGD) algorithm with update direction computed using a mini batch of 32 paraphrase pairs. Due to the large size of recurrent networks, the batch-size was limited to 32. We train the models for approximately 150 hours using multiple GPU machines (Tesla K20m, and Tesla K80).

We use *Theano* (Bergstra et al., 2011) for all our experiments. We use RNN templates provided by the *GroundHog* library[2]. For training, we use the *Adadelta* learning scheme (Zeiler, 2012) with ρ as 0.95 and eps as 1e-6. We use early stopping to prevent overfitting.

We use a beam search algorithm to generate optimal paraphrases by exploiting the trained models in the testing phase (Sutskever et al., 2014). We also create a SMT model to compare the performance of the proposed models. We use the *Moses* package (Koehn et al., 2007) for this purpose, which uses a phrase-based approach by combining a translation model and a language model to generate paraphrases. We use the default settings to create the SMT model.

4.3 Evaluation and Analysis

4.3.1 Automatic Evaluation

To quantitatively evaluate the performance of our paraphrase generation models, we use two well-known automatic metrics for machine translation evaluation: BLEU (Papineni et al., 2002) and METEOR (Lavie and Agarwal, 2007). Previous work has shown that these metrics can perform well for the paraphrase recognition task (Madnani et al., 2012) and correlate well with human judgments in evaluating generated paraphrases (Wubben et al., 2010). BLEU considers exact matching between target paraphrases and system generated paraphrases by considering n-gram overlaps. Meanwhile, METEOR improves upon this measure via stemming and synonymy using WordNet. We compute BLEU scores with jBLEU V0.1.1 (an exact reimplementation of NIST's mteval-v13.pl without tokenization) and METEOR scores using METEOR V1.4 with all default settings (Clark et al., 2011).

Table 1 shows the average BLEU and METEOR scores for the NCPG models considering the source and the target paraphrases as references to the system generated paraphrases. The input/prediction level for all models are denoted in parenthesis. *Moses* is the word-level statistical paraphrase generation model trained using the Moses package. *Source-Target* refers to the scores computed between the source and the target paraphrase pairs of the test set, because the source text is also a paraphrase of the target text. This can essentially serve as an upper bound of the paraphrasing scores (Wubben et al., 2010).

Our results show that all NCPG models perform relatively better than *Source-Target* in terms of BLEU scores. Similar trend is also seen for METEOR scores. We also observe that *Moses* obtains the highest scores, which is expected because Moses uses an additional monolingual training corpus of 418M words that was not used to train our NCPG models. Moreover, as BLEU and METEOR scores consider the number of word/synonym overlaps between the source and target paraphrase pairs, our qualitative evaluation (reported in the next subsection) reveals that Moses often repeats the source text as the generated target paraphrases and achieves higher scores for exact matching. This phenomenon is also evident from the *Source-Target* scores, which denote that models can achieve lower BLEU/METEOR scores even though they generate better quality paraphrases.

The results also reveal that the attention-based NCPG models mostly outperform the RNN encoder-decoder models, and char-level NCPG models perform considerably better than their word-level counterparts. Qualitative analysis revealed that word-level NCPG models largely suffered from OOV issues

---

[2]https://github.com/lisa-groundhog/GroundHog

while char-level models could efficiently deal with this problem. This is a noteworthy achievement because our character-level models do not require language-dependent grammatical pre-processing and they learn from efficient encoding of character sequences while being tolerant to spelling errors, a very common occurrence in clinical documents. We hypothesize that the results of the char-level models would further improve if pre-trained character embeddings based on a large background clinical corpus (e.g. biomedical literature corpus such as PubMed Central[3]) can be used during training.

Model	BLEU	METEOR
NCPG-1 (Word)	18.8	30.5
NCPG-1 (Char)	31.3	32.1
NCPG-2 (Word)	24.0	31.0
NCPG-2 (Char)	30.1	32.3
Moses	50.2	47.0
Source-Target	14.6	26.2

Table 1: Automatic evaluation scores for all models.

4.3.2 Human Evaluation

Automatic evaluation of paraphrasing is difficult as BLEU and METEOR can capture the textual similarity while disregarding the novelty of the generated paraphrases (Callison-Burch et al., 2008). Hence, we conduct human evaluation to qualitatively evaluate the performance of our NCPG models. We use a methodology derived from Wubben et al. (2010) for this purpose. Five judges (familiar with the clinical domain) evaluated the quality of a randomly selected subset (2%) of the paraphrases from the test set using three criteria: 1) *semantic relatedness:* whether the overall meaning is preserved in the paraphrase, 2) *novelty*[4]: if the paraphrase is considerably different from the source text, and 3) *grammaticality:* if the paraphrase is syntactically correct and fluent. The judges were presented with the source and the target text along with the system generated paraphrases. Note that, the target text is considered as one of many candidate paraphrases of the source text. For each of the criteria, the judges assigned an integer score between 1 (very poor) and 5 (very good) to each paraphrase. System settings and model identities were not disclosed to the judges during evaluation.

Table 2 shows the average quality scores for all models. These results demonstrate that on average, our attention-based models (*NCPG-2*) outperform the *NCPG-1* models, and char-level models perform better than word-level models in terms of semantic relatedness and grammaticality while underperforming in terms of novelty. Furthermore, our word-level NCPG models perform better than *Moses* in terms of novelty (up to 22% improvement) as *Moses* often generates the same paraphrase as the source sequence. These results show that on average, our proposed models perform on par with *Moses* and *Source-Target*.

Model	Meaning	Novelty	Grammaticality	Average
NCPG-1 (Word)	3.23	2.65	3.78	3.22
NCPG-1 (Char)	3.28	2.23	4.02	3.18
NCPG-2 (Word)	3.18	2.90	3.84	3.31
NCPG-2 (Char)	3.36	2.30	3.95	3.20
Moses	3.83	2.38	4.06	3.42
Source-Target	3.47	2.90	4.16	3.51

Table 2: Human evaluation scores for all models.

---

[3] http://www.ncbi.nlm.nih.gov/pmc/
[4] Novelty is inherently dependent on semantic relatedness because new words that do not preserve the overall meaning of the source text are undesirable.

4.3.3   Example Paraphrases

Table 3 presents some example source and target texts with corresponding system generated paraphrases from our models. These examples suggest that the word-level NCPG models generate better quality clinical paraphrases similar to *Moses*[5]. Also, char-level NCPG models perform well in generating comparable paraphrase texts. This confirms the effectiveness of the proposed NCPG models. Note that our curated corpus is mostly built on lexical and phrasal paraphrases. In future, we plan to construct a sentence-level parallel clinical paraphrase corpus to test the performance of our NCPG models for sentential paraphrasing.

Source:	Target:
contagious diseases	communicable diseases
Model	**Paraphrase**
NCPG-1 (Word)	habitat
NCPG-1 (Char)	contact diseases
NCPG-2 (Word)	an infectious disease
NCPG-2 (Char)	the diseases
Moses	infectious diseases
Source:	**Target:**
secondary malignant neoplasm of spleen	secondary malignant deposit to spleen
Model	**Paraphrase**
NCPG-1 (Word)	secondary cancer of spleen
NCPG-1 (Char)	separation of spleen
NCPG-2 (Word)	secondary malignant neoplasm of spleen
NCPG-2 (Char)	secondary malignant neoplasm
Moses	metastatic ca spleen
Source:	**Target:**
abdominal lymph node structure	intraabdominal lymph node
Model	**Paraphrase**
NCPG-1 (Word)	abdominal lymph node
NCPG-1 (Char)	abdominal lymph nodes
NCPG-2 (Word)	abdominal lymph nodes
NCPG-2 (Char)	abdominal lymph
Moses	retroperitoneal node sructure

Table 3: Paraphrase examples.

5   Conclusion and Future Work

In this paper, we proposed a novel approach called *neural clinical paraphrase generation* by using the monolingual NMT principles. We used an attention-based bidirectional RNN encoder-decoder framework to build an end-to-end architecture to accomplish the task by considering both word-level and char-level computations. To the best of our knowledge, this work is the first that uses attention-based RNNs for clinical paraphrase generation and also proposes an end-to-end character-level modeling for this task. Extensive automatic and human evaluation on a large curated parallel corpus demonstrated that the proposed NCPG models can outperform an RNN encoder-decoder based strong baseline while performing on par with the traditional SMT models. We also showed that character-based NCPG models can often outperform word-level models to remedy the OOV issues while generating paraphrases. In future, we will experiment with alternative structures for character-level RNN-based (Bojanowski et al., 2015) neural paraphrase generation architectures, and exploit a larger monolingual clinical paraphrase corpus to enhance the performance of our models.

Acknowledgment

The authors would like to thank the anonymous reviewers for their valuable comments and feedback.

---

[5]Note *Moses* has misspelled the word "structure" in the last example.

References

I. Androutsopoulos and P. Malakasiotis. 2010. A Survey of Paraphrasing and Textual Entailment Methods. *Journal of Artificial Intelligence Research*, 38(1):135–187.

D. Bahdanau, K. Cho, and Y. Bengio. 2015. Neural Machine Translation by Jointly Learning to Align and Translate. In *Proceedings of ICLR*, pages 1–15.

C. Bannard and C. Callison-Burch. 2005. Paraphrasing with Bilingual Parallel Corpora. In *Proceedings of ACL*, pages 597–604.

Y. Bengio, P. Simard, and P. Frasconi. 1994. Learning Long-Term Dependencies with Gradient Descent is Difficult. *IEEE Transactions on Neural Networks*, 5(2):157–166.

J. Bergstra, F. Bastien, O. Breuleux, P. Lamblin, R. Pascanu, O. Delalleau, G. Desjardins, D. Warde-Farley, I. Goodfellow, A. Bergeron, et al. 2011. Theano: Deep Learning on GPUs with Python. In *NIPS 2011, BigLearning Workshop, Granada, Spain*.

P. Bojanowski, A. Joulin, and T. Mikolov. 2015. Alternative structures for character-level RNNs. In *arXiv:1511.06303 [cs.LG]*.

C. Callison-Burch, T. Cohn, and M. Lapata. 2008. ParaMetric: An Automatic Evaluation Metric for Paraphrasing. In *Proceedings of COLING*, pages 97–104.

K. Cho, B. van Merrienboer, D. Bahdanau, and Y. Bengio. 2014a. On the Properties of Neural Machine Translation: Encoder–Decoder Approaches. In *Proceedings of SSST-8, Eighth Workshop on Syntax, Semantics and Structure in Statistical Translation*, pages 103–111.

K. Cho, B. van Merrienboer, C. Gulcehre, D. Bahdanau, F. Bougares, H. Schwenk, and Y. Bengio. 2014b. Learning Phrase Representations using RNN Encoder–Decoder for Statistical Machine Translation. In *Proceedings of EMNLP*, pages 1724–1734.

J. Chung, K. Cho, and Y. Bengio. 2016. A Character-level Decoder without Explicit Segmentation for Neural Machine Translation. In *arXiv:1603.06147 [cs.CL]*.

J. H. Clark, C. Dyer, A. Lavie, and N. A. Smith. 2011. Better Hypothesis Testing for Statistical Machine Translation: Controlling for Optimizer Instability. In *Proceedings of ACL-HLT*, pages 176–181.

R. Cornet and N. de Keizer. 2008. Forty Years of SNOMED: A Literature Review. *BMC Medical Informatics and Decision Making*, 8(S-1):S2:1–7.

M. R. Costa-JussÃ and J. A. R. Fonollosa. 2016. Character-based Neural Machine Translation. In *arXiv:1603.00810 [cs.CL]*.

L. Deléger and P. Zweigenbaum. 2009. Extracting Lay Paraphrases of Specialized Expressions from Monolingual Comparable Medical Corpora. In *Proceedings of the 2nd Workshop on Building and Using Comparable Corpora: From Parallel to Non-parallel Corpora*, pages 2–10.

N. Elhadad and K. Sutaria. 2007. Mining a Lexicon of Technical Terms and Lay Equivalents. In *Proceedings of the Workshop on BioNLP*, pages 49–56.

A. Graves. 2013. Generating Sequences With Recurrent Neural Networks. In *arXiv:1308.0850 [cs.NE]*.

S. Hassan, A. Csomai, C. Banea, R. Sinha, and R. Mihalcea. 2007. UNT: SubFinder: Combining Knowledge Sources for Automatic Lexical Substitution. In *Proceedings of SemEval*, pages 410–413.

S. Hochreiter and J. Schmidhuber. 1997. Long Short-Term Memory. *Neural Computation*, 9(8):1735–1780.

S. Jean, K. Cho, R. Memisevic, and Y. Bengio. 2015. On Using Very Large Target Vocabulary for Neural Machine Translation. In *Proceedings of ACL*, pages 1–10.

N. Kalchbrenner and P. Blunsom. 2013. Recurrent Continuous Translation Models. In *Proceedings of EMNLP*, pages 1700–1709.

Y. Kim, Y. Jernite, D. Sontag, and A. M. Rush. 2015. Character-Aware Neural Language Models. In *arXiv:1508.06615 [cs.CL]*.

P. Koehn, F. J. Och, and D. Marcu. 2003. Statistical Phrase-based Translation. In *Proceedings of NAACL-HLT*, pages 48–54.

P. Koehn, H. Hoang, A. Birch, C. Callison-Burch, M. Federico, N. Bertoldi, B. Cowan, W. Shen, C. Moran, R. Zens, C. Dyer, O. Bojar, A. Constantin, and E. Herbst. 2007. Moses: Open Source Toolkit for Statistical Machine Translation. In *Proceedings of ACL Interactive Poster and Demo. Sessions*, pages 177–180.

P. Koehn. 2010. *Statistical Machine Translation*. Cambridge University Press, New York, NY, USA.

R. Kozlowski, K. F. McCoy, and K. Vijay-Shanker. 2003. Generation of Single-sentence Paraphrases from Predicate/Argument Structure Using Lexico-grammatical Resources. In *Proceedings of the 2nd International Workshop on Paraphrasing*, pages 1–8.

A. Lavie and A. Agarwal. 2007. METEOR: An Automatic Metric for MT Evaluation with High Levels of Correlation with Human Judgments. In *Proceedings of the Second Workshop on Statistical Machine Translation*, pages 228–231.

D. Lindberg, B. Humphreys, and A. McCray. 1993. The Unified Medical Language System. *Methods of Information in Medicine*, 32(4):281–291.

W. Ling, I. Trancoso, C. Dyer, and A. W. Black. 2015. Character-based Neural Machine Translation. In *arXiv:1511.04586 [cs.CL]*.

T. Luong, H. Pham, and C. D. Manning. 2015a. Effective Approaches to Attention-based Neural Machine Translation. In *Proceedings of EMNLP*, pages 1412–1421.

T. Luong, I. Sutskever, Q. V. Le, O. Vinyals, and W. Zaremba. 2015b. Addressing the Rare Word Problem in Neural Machine Translation. In *Proceedings of ACL-IJCNLP*, pages 11–19.

N. Madnani and B. J. Dorr. 2010. Generating Phrasal and Sentential Paraphrases: A Survey of Data-driven Methods. *Computational Linguistics*, 36(3):341–387.

N. Madnani, J. Tetreault, and M. Chodorow. 2012. Re-examining Machine Translation Metrics for Paraphrase Identification. In *Proceedings of NAACL-HLT*, pages 182–190.

K. R. McKeown. 1983. Paraphrasing Questions Using Given and New Information. *Computational Linguistics*, 9(1):1–10.

K. Papineni, S. Roukos, T. Ward, and W. Zhu. 2002. BLEU: a Method for Automatic Evaluation of Machine Translation. In *Proceedings of ACL*, pages 311–318.

E. Pavlick, J. Ganitkevitch, T. P. Chan, X. Yao, B. Van Durme, and C. Callison-Burch. 2015a. Domain-specific paraphrase extraction. In *Proceedings of ACL-IJCNLP*, pages 57–62, Beijing, China.

E. Pavlick, P. Rastogi, J. Ganitkevitch, B. Van Durme, and C. Callison-Burch. 2015b. PPDB 2.0: Better paraphrase ranking, fine-grained entailment relations, word embeddings, and style classification. In *Proceedings of ACL-IJCNLP)*, pages 425–430.

E. Prud'hommeaux and B. Roark. 2015. Graph-Based Word Alignment for Clinical Language Evaluation. *Computational Linguistics*, 41(4):549–578.

C. Quirk, C. Brockett, and W. Dolan. 2004. Monolingual Machine Translation for Paraphrase Generation. In *Proceedings of EMNLP*, pages 142–149.

M. Schuster and K.K. Paliwal. 1997. Bidirectional Recurrent Neural Networks. *IEEE Transactions on Signal Processing*, 45(11):2673–2681.

R. Socher, E. H. Huang, J. Pennington, A. Y. Ng, and C. D. Manning. 2011. Dynamic Pooling and Unfolding Recursive Autoencoders for Paraphrase Detection. In *Advances in Neural Information Processing Systems*, pages 1–9.

A. Sperduti. 2015. Equivalence Results between Feedforward and Recurrent Neural Networks for Sequences. In *Proceedings of IJCAI*, pages 3827–3833.

I. Sutskever, J. Martens, and G. E. Hinton. 2011. Generating Text with Recurrent Neural Networks. In *Proceedings of ICML*, pages 1017–1024.

I. Sutskever, O. Vinyals, and Q. V. Le. 2014. Sequence to Sequence Learning with Neural Networks. In *Annual Conference on Neural Information Processing Systems*, pages 3104–3112.

C. Wang, L. Cao, and B. Zhou. 2015. Medical Synonym Extraction with Concept Space Models. In *Proceedings of IJCAI*, pages 989–995.

S. Wubben, A. van den Bosch, and E. Krahmer. 2010. Paraphrase Generation As Monolingual Translation: Data and Evaluation. In *Proceedings of INLG*, pages 203–207.

W. Yin and H. Schütze. 2015. Convolutional Neural Network for Paraphrase Identification. In *Proceedings of NAACL-HLT*, pages 901–911.

M. D. Zeiler. 2012. ADADELTA: An Adaptive Learning Rate Method. In *arXiv:1212.5701 [cs.LG]*.

S. Zhao, C. Niu, M. Zhou, T. Liu, and S. Li. 2008. Combining Multiple Resources to Improve SMT-based Paraphrasing Model. In *Proceedings of ACL-HLT*, pages 1021–1029.

S. Zhao, X. Lan, T. Liu, and S. Li. 2009. Application-driven Statistical Paraphrase Generation. In *Proceedings of ACL-IJCNLP*, pages 834–842.

S. Zhao, H. Wang, X. Lan, and T. Liu. 2010. Leveraging Multiple MT Engines for Paraphrase Generation. In *Proceedings of COLING*, pages 1326–1334.

Assessing the Corpus Size vs. Similarity Trade-off
for Word Embeddings in Clinical NLP

Kirk Roberts
School of Biomedical Informatics
University of Texas Health Science Center at Houston
Houston, TX, USA
`kirk.roberts@uth.tmc.edu`

Abstract

The proliferation of deep learning methods in natural language processing (NLP) and the large amounts of data they often require stands in stark contrast to the relatively data-poor clinical NLP domain. In particular, large text corpora are necessary to build high-quality word embeddings, yet often large corpora that are suitably representative of the target clinical data are unavailable. This forces a choice between building embeddings from small clinical corpora and less representative, larger corpora. This paper explores this trade-off, as well as intermediate compromise solutions. Two standard clinical NLP tasks (the i2b2 2010 concept and assertion tasks) are evaluated with commonly used deep learning models (recurrent neural networks and convolutional neural networks) using a set of six corpora ranging from the target i2b2 data to large open-domain datasets. While combinations of corpora are generally found to work best, the single-best corpus is generally task-dependent.

1 Introduction

The use of vector representations in natural language processing (NLP) has a solid foundation (Turian et al., 2010; Collobert et al., 2011). These enable dense representations that often encode semantic properties and are particularly useful for machine learning tasks as an alternative to extremely sparse, "one-hot" vocabulary-length vector representations. Many ways of building these vectors exist, including random indexing (Sahlgren, 2006), clustering (Brown et al., 1992), regression (Pennington et al., 2014), and neural (Mikolov et al., 2013) methods. This paper focuses on the last such type of vector representation, often referred to as *embeddings*, and exemplified by the popular method `word2vec` (Mikolov et al., 2013).

Embeddings are particularly useful in neural network architectures, which due to their heavy use of matrix multiplication typically favor low-dimensional, dense representation. In particular, neural network models that utilize multiple layers of operations to find abstractions in the data (collectively referred to as deep learning models) are a natural fit for these dense semantic representations.

In what is typically a semi-supervised process, word embeddings are generated from a large, representative sample of data. Then, a smaller manually annotated sample is used to train the deep learning models. However, this results in a common problem for clinical NLP: large representative corpora (at least comparable to those used in much open-domain NLP research) are not often available for building these embeddings. This is due to the significant restrictions on the use of electronic health record (EHR) data, especially narrative notes, for research purposes. Clinical NLP researchers and practitioners are often then left with a trade-off: using a small-but-representative corpus versus a large-but-unrepresentative corpus. The former may not be large enough to properly capture the necessary semantics, while the latter might not be representative enough to capture the semantics of some of the most important words in the corpus. For instance, a large open-domain corpus might associate the abbreviation *ms* with *millisecond* (or *Mississippi*) rather than *multiple sclerosis* (or *mitral stenosis*).

In theory, one could simply experiment with multiple corpora to see what works best for a given task. But in practice this may be overly burdensome, especially in the context of deep learning models that have many, many other important parameters and architectural choices to consider, in addition to their

Proceedings of the Clinical Natural Language Processing Workshop,
pages 54–63, Osaka, Japan, December 11-17 2016.

long training times. What would be useful, then, is some intuitive notion or rule-of-thumb on what corpora to use for building word embeddings for clinical NLP. From a practical point-of-view, one can see two ideal scenarios:

1. A small target corpus (several hundred or a few thousand documents) that is highly representative of the annotated notes in the clinical NLP task (possibly including the annotated notes themselves).

2. A large corpus (millions of documents) that is completely general-purpose (likely not containing clinical note text at all).

If the first scenario were to result in optimal system performance, this would be quite easy for the clinical NLP practitioner: for each NLP task, generate a set of embeddings specific to the corpus. The second scenario is even easier: simply use an "off-the-shelf" set of word embeddings. However, there are many possible compromise solutions between these two extremes. For example, a medium-size corpus of clinical notes from a different corpus, or a large corpus of scientific articles, or even a combination of two or more of these. The goal of this paper is to explore this size vs. similarity trade-off, specifically for clinical NLP purposes. A handful of corpora ranging from a small target corpus to a large general-purpose corpus are used to build embeddings. Experiments using two common deep learning models in combination with two standard clinical NLP datasets are used to evaluate this trade-off.

The remainder of this paper is organized as follows. Section 2 describes related work with word embeddings, including its use in clinical NLP. Section 3 describes the tasks used to evaluate the embeddings. Section 4 describes the datasets used to generate the embeddings. Section 5 describes the experimental setup, including the parameters for generating the word embeddings as well as the parameters for the deep learning models. Section 6 shows the results of the experiments. Section 7 discusses the implications, with some practical considerations.

2 Related Work

As mentioned above, there are various types of word vector representations for use in NLP (Brown et al., 1992; Sahlgren, 2006; Mikolov et al., 2013; Pennington et al., 2014). By themselves, these are well-known to be easily integrateable into common NLP tasks (Turian et al., 2010; Collobert et al., 2011). Generally, the best types of representations have semantic properties, notably that synonyms are nearby in vector space, and certain types of vector operations (addition and subtraction) roughly correspond to semantic operations. This largely holds for neural word embeddings, which allow for the induction of additional semantic properties, such as hypernymy relations (Fu et al., 2014). As embeddings become more and more important in NLP, work continues on analyzing their usefulness, such as how to interpret specific vector dimensions (Luo et al., 2015), but most work focuses on applying embeddings to well-defined NLP tasks.

Further, the increased importance of deep learning methods in NLP has resulted in a significant number of uses of embeddings to represent words. Wang and Manning (2013) help clarify the relationship between embeddings and deep learning models: these models excel with low-dimensional, continuous representations, but offer no benefit over more traditional models like conditional random fields (CRF) (Lafferty et al., 2001) when used with high-dimensional, discrete representations. Embeddings for NLP are commonly used in sequence classification tasks such as part-of-speech tagging and chunking (Huang et al., 2015), named entity recognition (Chiu and Nichols, 2016; Lample et al., 2016), and semantic role labeling (Zhou and Xu, 2015). Typically, these sequence models are based on recurrent neural networks (RNN). Classification models, on the other hand, are often based on convolutional neural networks (CNN). These models are more adept at picking out a relevant piece of information in a relatively long span of text, and so are often used for sentence classification (Kim, 2014; Zhang and Wallace, 2016), or sentiment and topic prediction (Zhang et al., 2015). Note that many other deep learning methods are possible with embeddings, such as sentiment classification with recursive autoencoders (Socher et al., 2011), but this paper focuses on the use of RNNs and CNNs specifically for clinical NLP.

While less explored than the open domain, research exists on the uses of word embeddings for clinical NLP (though less so in the context of a deep learning model). Several non-neural vector representations

3. Echocardiogram on **DATE[Nov 6 2007] , showed ejection fraction of 55% , mild mitral insufficiency , and 1+ tricuspid insufficiency with mild pulmonary hypertension .
DERMOPLAST TOPICAL TP Q12H PRN Pain DOCUSATE SODIUM 100 MG PO BID PRN Constipation IBUPROFEN 400-600 MG PO Q6H PRN Pain
The patient is struggling to breathe at this time , and she is tachypneic , and she might have to be intubated right now but ; however , the patient 's family did not wish the patient to be intubated even after I explained to them that she could potentially die if she was not on a breathing machine ; but however , the patient 's family stressed to me again and wished that they do not want her mother to be on a breathing machine .
The patient had headache that was relieved only with oxycodone . A CT scan of the head showed microvascular ischemic changes . A followup MRI which also showed similar changes . This was most likely due to her multiple myeloma with hyperviscosity .

Table 1: Examples of concepts (**Problem**, **Treatment**, and Test) from the i2b2 2010 corpus.

have been used for named entity recognition style tasks, notably random indexing (Jonnalagadda et al., 2012; Henriksson et al., 2014). Most uses of neural embeddings have likewise been through non-deep learning models. Wu et al. (2015) explored different feature representations for embeddings, showing that for CRFs both binarized and distributed prototype embeddings (Guo et al., 2014) out-performed the raw embeddings. Related, but outside of clinical NLP, Tang et al. (2014) study the use of word representations, including embeddings, for gene/protein NER, also within the context of CRF features.

Finally, there has been some study on the use of multiple word embeddings in the context of deep learning models. Luo et al. (2014) learn new task-specific embeddings from multiple pre-trained embeddings for the purpose of search ranking and text similarity. Yin and Schütze (2015) treat multiple word embeddings as different channels in a CNN. This achieves great performance, but requires all the embeddings be of the same dimension. In contrast, the method in this paper uses simple concatenation, which does not require equal dimensions, but Yin and Schütze (2015) may still have some desirable semantic properties. Finally, Zhang et al. (2016) proposes a multi-group norm constraint CNN (MGNC-CNN) that separates the convolutional layers for different sets of embeddings. This model also has a lot of promise, but it beyond the scope of this work. Additionally, all of these multi-embedding models have focused on CNNs, while it is not clear whether Yin and Schütze (2015) or Zhang et al. (2016) could be successfully applied to RNNs. However, the focus in this paper is on devising an intuition behind choosing the right sets of embeddings (or ideally, only one set of embeddings).

3 Tasks

Two common clinical NLP tasks are considered: sequence classification and multi-class text classification. While sequence classification is often a type of multi-class text classification (if there is more than one type of phrase to be recognized), it nonetheless is often treated differently in regards to the "default" machine learning algorithm (i.e., SVM vs. CRF). For each type of task, a specific task from the i2b2 2010 Shared Task (Uzuner et al., 2011b) is selected for the experiments. While the deep learning-based models used for each task are mentioned here, Section 5 contains more details on the actual implementations.

3.1 Sequence Classification

Word embeddings for sequence classification are evaluated using the i2b2 2010 concept recognition task. A medical concept in this task is a problem (e.g., disease or symptom), treatment (e.g., drug or therapeutic procedure), or test (e.g., diagnostic procedure). This is an especially difficult problem in clinical NLP due to the compact nature of text in EHR notes. Table 1 shows examples of different concept types from the i2b2 2010 corpus, while Table 2 shows their distributions in the train and test sets.

To model concept recognition, a bi-directional recurrent neural network (RNN) using long short-term memory (LSTM) units (Hochreiter and Schmidhuber, 1997) is used. LSTM-RNNs are heavily used in named entity recognition and other sequence-based NLP tasks (Hammerton, 2003; Huang et al., 2015; Zhou and Xu, 2015; Chiu and Nichols, 2016; Lample et al., 2016).

	Train Set	Test Set	Total
Documents	349	477	826
Concepts	27,831	45,009	72,840
Problems	11,967	18,550	30,517
Treatments	8,496	13,560	22,056
Tests	7,368	12,899	20,267

Table 2: Frequencies of concept types in the i2b2 2010 corpus.

Present	... a short - term temporary measure , and after her pneumonia gets better ... ... demonstrating a low fibrinogen , positive D-dimer , and ... ... admitted with vomiting and fever and found to have urinary tract infection ...
Absent	... patient 's left back pain was evaluated and ruled out for MI and the back pain ... His neck was supple with no jugular venous distention or thyromegaly . He denied any fevers , chills , or night sweats .
Hypothetical	The patient was instructed to report any new or increased shortness of breath ... The patient is to expect some blood in his urine for the first couple of days . ... her steroid inhalers and PO prednisone for COPD exacerbation .
Possible	... who came to the hospital with what appears to be acute coronary syndrome . ... multiple bilateral pulmonary nodules compatible with inflammatory disease . The patient did not have any EKG changes consistent with hyperkalemia .
Conditional	... chest tightness (pressure) approximately every three months with stress . He reports severe dyspnea on exertion . ... pt slightly lightheaded and with increased HR when getting up out of bed .
Associated with Someone Else	She has no family history of gallbladder or pancreatic disease . His mother and father both died secondary to myocardial infarction . The patient's sister has a history of cervical cancer .

Table 3: Examples of assertions types for Problems from the i2b2 2010 corpus.

3.2 Multi-class Text Classification

Word embeddings for multi-class text classification are evaluated using the i2b2 2010 assertion task. An assertion is a belief state about a medical problem (present, absent, hypothetical, etc.). This is especially important in clinical NLP as diagnoses are often ruled out or speculated about during the diagnostic process. Table 3 shows examples of different assertion types from the i2b2 2010 corpus, while Table 4 shows their distributions in the train and test sets.

To model assertion classification, a 2-layer convolutional neural network (CNN) with a max-pooling layer and softmax classifier is used. While more noteworthy for imaging tasks, CNNs have been heavily utilized in text classification as well (Collobert et al., 2011; Kim, 2014; Zhang et al., 2015; Zhang and Wallace, 2016).

4 Data

Six datasets are utilized for generating word vectors (see Table 5):

i2b2 is the "target" dataset. This is a combination of multiple years worth of i2b2 shared tasks: 2010 (Uzuner et al., 2011b), 2011 (Uzuner et al., 2011a), and 2012 (Uzuner et al., 2013) tasks. However, the vast majority come from the same data pull(s) used to build the training and testing data (87%) for the 2010 tasks described in Section 3. This dataset corresponds to the first ideal scenario described above, since it would be practical if this data alone would be sufficient to generate optimal word embeddings as additional corpora would never be needed. However, as is often the case in practice, far less data is available in this dataset compared to what is typically used to generate word embeddings.

	Train Set	Test Set	Total
Documents	349	477	826
Problems	11,967	18,550	30,517
Present	8,052	13,025	21,077
Absent	2,535	3,609	6,144
Hypothetical	651	883	1,534
Possible	535	717	1,252
Conditional	103	171	274
Associated with Someone Else	92	145	237

Table 4: Frequencies of assertion types in the i2b2 2010 corpus.

MIMIC3 (Johnson et al., 2016) is a freely-accessible database of intensive care unit (ICU) encounters from a large hospital. It is significantly larger than the i2b2 dataset, and some of the i2b2 data was even drawn from MIMIC-II. MIMIC-III represents the next-best case scenario to having a large clinical target dataset: it is both large and fairly similar to the i2b2 data. MIMIC is commonly used to generate word embeddings for clinical NLP, but its exact utility in comparison to the target dataset is rarely, if ever, measured.

MEDLINE is a collection of scientific article abstracts maintained by the National Library of Medicine. While a large dataset, these are not clinical notes and lack many of the peculiarities of clinical notes (e.g., abbreviations, telegraphic text). Further, while clinical notes are written by clinicians largely to communicate with other clinicians, MEDLINE abstracts are written by researchers largely to communicate with other researchers. However, MEDLINE does discuss almost all the diseases, conditions, treatments, and techniques that are described in clinical notes.

WebMD Forum is a collection of forum posts on the WebMD Community[1]. The forum posts are written largely by health consumers, who are known to write health-related text quite differently than clinicians (Roberts and Demner-Fushman, 2016). This dataset is intended to represent a small-to-medium-size medically-related corpus that is nonetheless quite different from clinical notes.

Wikipedia is a large, online encyclopedia. Wikipedia has extensive coverage of medical topics, but also many other topics as well. Wikipedia represents the other best-case scenario for generating word embeddings: if near-optimal performance could be obtained using such a general corpus, it could be used in all experiments without the need to generate new word embeddings for each task.

Gigaword is a large newswire corpus (Parker et al., 2009). It has extensive coverage of topics that typically dominate the news media, including politics and sports, but its coverage of medicine is largely limited to newsworthy studies and announcements. Gigaword represents a control corpus: it should be less useful than Wikipedia, but if it were to be beneficial then one could argue that using several arbitrary corpora simultaneously (like an ensemble) is useful simply to provide multiple views of each word, or even just more free parameters for the neural network to work with.

Instead of creating word embeddings for each combination of corpora, the embeddings are built for each individual corpus independently. This has several advantages. First, it prevents the smaller, more similar corpora from being "drowned out" by the larger, more distant corpora. Second, it dramatically reduces the time needed to produce the embeddings since only N embeddings are needed. Third, providing the neural networks with multiple sets of embeddings allows for a kind of domain adaptation to take place: the networks can learn to take different information from different corpora, which it would not be able to do with a single, unified embedding vector built from all the data. As mentioned above, multi-embedding models have been utilized for neural networks before. The implementation here is intentionally one of the simplest forms of embedding combinations: simple concatenation of the em-

---

[1]http://exchanges.webmd.com/

Corpus	# Documents	# Sentences	# Tokens	*% diabetes*	*% myocardial*	*% tumor*
i2b2	3k	158k	1.7m	2.9e-4%	2.4e-4%	1.3e-4%
MIMIC	876k	17m	366m	1.0e-4%	1.2e-4%	9.1e-5%
MEDLINE	24m	138m	3.7b	2.2e-4%	1.5e-5%	7.9e-4%
WebMD	232k	1.5m	24m	1.3e-4%	4.5e-7%	3.4e-5%
Wikipedia	4.8m	96m	2.1b	7.0e-6%	1.0e-6%	1.1e-5%
Gigaword	8.5m	169m	4.1b	9.3e-6%	N/A	7.5e-6%

Table 5: Basic corpus statistics, including the proportion of three important clinical terms (*diabetes*, *myocardial*, *tumor*) to illustrate how representative each corpus is of clinical text. Note that this excludes common clinical abbreviations (e.g., *dm* or *dm2* for *diabetes*). "N/A" indicates the word was not in the top 100k terms and thus not included in the embeddings.

bedding vectors. Other methods are possible (Zhang et al., 2016), but it is unclear whether these more specialized methods would produce results as generalizable as simple vector concatenation.

5 Experimental Setup

Both word embeddings and deep learning models have very many possible parameters that can impact downstream tasks. The following experimental description is by no means likely to be optimal for the tasks, but was made based on a combination of default parameters, conventional wisdom, and practical necessity. In some cases experiments were conducted to test parameter impact on the downstream tasks (mostly with the more crucial deep learning model parameters). See Section 7.1 for a discussion of the limitations of these experiments.

5.1 Word Vectors

Each corpus was pre-processed with tokenization and sentence segmentation. Case was removed. Numbers were altered to just the most significant digit (e.g., 929 becomes 900). Word occurring less than 5 times were changed to UNK. Finally, a maximum vocabulary of 100k word types was applied, keeping only the most frequent words. The numbers in Table 5 reflect these transformations. The gensim (Řehůřek and Sojka, 2010) version of word2vec was then applied to create 100-dimensional embeddings largely using default parameters (CBOW, α=0.025, 5-word window, 50 epochs).

5.2 Recurrent Neural Network

The RNN uses a bi-directional, 3-layer LSTM implemented in TensorFlow (Abadi et al., 2015). Each LSTM cell uses 256 hidden units. Dropout is set to 0.5. A maximum sequence length of 50 tokens per sentence is used, which includes 98.4% of the concepts in the test set. Of the 30k sentences in the training set, 5k are used as a validation set for early stopping, evaluated up to 100 training epochs. The i2b2 concepts are represented in IOB format.

5.3 Convolutional Neural Network

The CNN uses 2 convolutional layers with a ReLU activation followed by a max-pooling layer and a softmax classifier, again implemented in TensorFlow. Optimization is performed with the Adam algorithm. Filters of sizes 1, 2, 3, and 4 are used, each replicated 400 times. No dropout is used. A context window of 3 tokens around the problem's first token is used for a total input width of 7 tokens. Of the 12k problems in the training set, 1k are used as a validation set for early stopping, evaluated up to 300 training epochs.

6 Results

The results of the experiments are shown in Table 6 and Table 7.

Concept recognition is measured in precision, recall, and micro-averaged F_1-measure. The single best corpus for this task was the MIMIC data, which out-performed the target i2b2 corpus in F_1 by 2.7 points. It also outperformed the more general-purpose Wikipedia and Gigaword corpora in F_1 by 4.7 and 7.5

Corpus	P	R	F_1
i2b2	74.47	80.12	77.19
MIMIC	77.99	81.97	**79.93**
MEDLINE	76.64	82.83	79.61
WebMD	71.95	77.72	74.72
Wikipedia	72.40	78.25	75.21
Gigaword	71.64	76.98	74.22
Corpus combination, starting with i2b2			
+ MIMIC	78.30	82.86	80.52
+ MEDLINE	79.65	83.71	**81.63**
+ WebMD	79.10	83.99	81.47
+ Wikipedia	79.64	83.62	81.58
+ Gigaword	78.78	83.89	81.25

Table 6: Results for RNN-based concept recognition on the i2b2 2010 corpus, measured with precision (P), recall (R), and F_1-measure.

Corpus	Accuracy	P	A	H	B	C	O
i2b2	**91.29**	96.24	95.45	87.14	86.27	81.58	91.84
MIMIC	91.16	96.10	96.15	85.60	85.58	81.63	92.73
MEDLINE	90.98	95.70	95.92	86.59	90.51	85.25	91.59
WebMD	90.22	95.40	95.14	86.65	88.50	83.87	92.59
Wikipedia	90.36	95.71	94.84	86.05	86.37	82.35	96.06
Gigaword	90.33	95.59	95.39	86.11	85.60	78.38	94.44
Corpus combination, starting with i2b2							
+ MIMIC	91.26	96.29	95.36	86.44	86.58	86.96	85.48
+ MEDLINE	91.56	96.24	96.29	85.11	88.25	83.78	95.16
+ WebMD	91.39	96.46	95.43	85.76	85.79	86.75	89.33
+ Wikipedia	**91.58**	96.35	96.79	82.61	88.06	80.00	92.65
+ Gigaword	91.57	96.42	95.85	87.60	86.17	80.52	83.78

Table 7: Results for CNN-based assertion classification on the i2b2 2010 corpus, measured with accuracy, along with the F_1-measure for present (P), absent (A), hypothetical (H), possible (B), conditional (C), and associated with someone else (O).

points, respectively. MEDLINE did almost as well as MIMIC, while WebMD did poorly, only slightly better than Gigaword. Results improve when the corpora are combined. The best overall results are achieved by combining i2b2, MIMIC, and MEDLINE. Adding in the other corpora hurt performance slightly, by at most 0.4.

Assertion classification is measured in accuracy, with F_1-measures for the individual assertion type provided in Table 7. Unlike concepts, the single best corpus is the target i2b2 data. All other corpora performed close, with the worst performance being WebMD with a 1.1 point drop in accuracy. Only slight gains are seen by adding in other corpora, the best being all corpora except Gigaword for a 0.3 point improvement, but no substantial losses are seen either.

7 Discussion

It would first be useful to compare the results obtained above with the state-of-the-art methods for the concept and assertion tasks (Uzuner et al., 2011b). In both cases, the results are less than the best performing scores on the tasks, but they are quite close. The best concept RNN would have placed 6th overall (out of 22) and well above the median (77.78). The best assertion CNN would have done a bit worse, performing near the median. However, these models were built using not particularly well-optimized parameters and furthermore they only had access to word information. The many features used by participants in the i2b2 tasks (e.g., UMLS (Lindberg et al., 1993), NegEx (Chapman et al., 2001), and task-specific patterns) could be incorporated into these models for superior performance. The fact that near state-of-the-art performance is achieved without any medical knowledge or custom features speaks to the power of these models.

Regarding the ideal scenarios for embeddings discussed in the Introduction (target data only and general-purpose only embeddings), these turned out to unfortunately not be the best performing conditions. i2b2 was the single best corpus for assertions, but not for concepts. Rather, MIMIC and MEDLINE greatly outperformed i2b2 for concepts, and were only slightly behind for assertions. This difference is likely due to the small number of relevant phrases that indicate assertion types compared to the vast vocabulary of medical concepts. The second ideal scenario, using a general-purpose corpus only, performs quite poor as a single corpus for both tasks. If only one set of embeddings can be used, then, it seems a compromise corpus such as MIMIC might be best.

The multi-embedding experiments reveal an important point, however. Combining multiple sets of embeddings can help quite a bit (e.g., i2b2 + MIMIC + MEDLINE did 1.7 points better than MIMIC alone for concepts), while adding "bad" corpora only will only hurt slightly (adding a single corpus never brought the score down more than 0.3 points). Therefore, if it is not possible to perform many experiments with embeddings on the task data (a common case in many applied clinical NLP settings), using several corpora at once seems relatively safe.

7.1 Limitations

This paper seeks to identify best practices experimentally, so its limitations revolve around reasons why the results may not be generalizable. In this sense, the possible limitations are vast, including:

- Only two clinical NLP datasets were evaluated, so the results obtained here may vary greatly with other tasks.

- Only a handful of experiments (just less than a week of computing time) were conducted to optimize the parameters of the various models: every choice made in Section 5 may be suboptimal. This may have reduced performance inconsistently, changing the relative performance of the various corpora.

- As an explicit example of the above point, the use of 100-dimension embeddings is less than what is typically used (often 300). Since embedding combination was an intentional goal of this paper, the embedding dimensionality was kept small to reduce training time (e.g., 600 vs. 1800 dimensions for the final experiment).

- It would have been useful to evaluate on more corpora–clinical, medical, and general-purpose–to measure intra-domain variance.

- Multi-embedding methods (Yin and Schütze, 2015; Zhang et al., 2016) could have improved results over simple vector concatenation.

Despite the extent to which these limitations may reduce the ability to generalize the experiments, the results largely do match the intuitions gained elsewhere in NLP. For ensembles, for example, adding additional weak classifiers is more likely to have a strong positive effect than a strong negative effect, which is consistent with the above results.

8 Conclusion

This paper presented a series of experiments to evaluate the trade-off between small-but-representative corpora versus large-but-unrepresentative corpora for building word embeddings for clinical NLP tasks. Two standard clinical NLP tasks (i2b2 2010 concepts and assertions) were used in combination with two appropriate deep learning methods (RNNs and CNNs) to evaluate six text corpora of varying size and similarity to the target corpus. While using only the small target corpus or a large general-purpose corpus would have been ideal from a practical standpoint, empirically it was found that combining multiple corpora, especially a corpus like MIMIC, is the safest option for choosing embeddings.

References

Martín Abadi, Ashish Agarwal, Paul Barham, Eugene Brevdo, Zhifeng Chen, Craig Citro, Greg S. Corrado, Andy Davis, Jeffrey Dean, Matthieu Devin, Sanjay Ghemawat, Ian Goodfellow, Andrew Harp, Geoffrey Irving, Michael Isard, Yangqing Jia, Rafal Jozefowicz, Lukasz Kaiser, Manjunath Kudlur, Josh Levenberg, Dan Mané, Rajat Monga, Sherry Moore, Derek Murray, Chris Olah, Mike Schuster, Jonathon Shlens, Benoit Steiner, Ilya Sutskever, Kunal Talwar, Paul Tucker, Vincent Vanhoucke, Vijay Vasudevan, Fernanda Viégas, Oriol Vinyals, Pete Warden, Martin Wattenberg, Martin Wicke, Yuan Yu, and Xiaoqiang Zheng. 2015. TensorFlow: Large-Scale Machine Learning on Heterogeneous Systems. Software available from tensorflow.org.

PF Brown, PV deSouza, RL Mercer, VJ Della Pietra, and JC Lai. 1992. Class-Based n-gram Models of Natural Language. *Computational Linguistics*, pages 467–479.

Wendy W. Chapman, Will Bridewell, Paul Hanbury, Gregory F. Cooper, and Bruce G. Buchanan. 2001. A Simple Algorithm for Identifying Negated Findings and Diseases in Discharge Summaries. *Journal of Biomedical Informatics*, 34(5):301–310, October.

Jason P.C. Chiu and Eric Nichols. 2016. Named Entity Recognition with Bidirectional LSTM-CNNs. *Transactions of the Association for Computational Linguistics*, 4:357–370.

Ronan Collobert, Jason Weston, Léon Bottou, Michael Karlen, Koray Kavukcuoglu, and Pavel Kuksa. 2011. Natural Language Processing (Almost) from Scratch. *Journal of Machine Learning Research*, 12(Aug):2493–2537.

Ruiji Fu, Jiang Guo, Bing Qin, Wanxiang Che, Haifeng Wang, and Ting Liu. 2014. Learning Semantic Hierarchies via Word Embeddings. In *Proceedings of the 52nd Annual Meeting of the Association for Computational Linguistics*, pages 1199–1209.

Jiang Guo, Wanxiang Che, Haifeng Wang, and Ting Liu. 2014. Revisiting Embedding Features for Simple Semi-supervised Learning. In *Proceedings of the 2014 Conference on Empirical Methods in Natural Language Processing*, pages 110–120.

James Hammerton. 2003. Named Entity Recognition with Long Short-Term Memory. In *Proceedings of the Seventh Conference on Natural Language Learning*.

Aron Henriksson, Hercules Dalianis, and Stewart Kowalski. 2014. Generating features for named entity recognition by learning prototypes in semantic space: The case of de-identifying health records. In *Proceedings of the IEEE Conference on Bioinformatics and Biomedicine*, pages 450–457.

Sepp Hochreiter and Jurgen Schmidhuber. 1997. Long short-term memory. *Neural Computation*, 9(8):1735–1780.

Zhiheng Huang, Wei Xu, and Kai Yu. 2015. Bidirectional LSTM-CRF Models for Sequence Tagging. arXiv:1508.01991.

Alistair E.W. Johnson, Tom J. Pollard, Lu Shen, Li wei H. Lehman, Mengling Feng, Mohammad Ghassemi, Benjamin Moody, Peter Szolovits, Leo Anthony Celi, , and Roger G. Mark. 2016. MIMIC-III, a freely accessible critical care database. *Scientific Data*, 3:160035.

Siddhartha Jonnalagadda, Trevor Cohen, Stephen Wu, and Graciela Gonzalez. 2012. Enhancing clinical concept extraction with distributional semantics. *Journal of Biomedical Informatics*, 45(1):129–140.

Yoon Kim. 2014. Convolutional Neural Networks for Sentence Classification. In *Proceedings of the 2014 Conference on Empirical Methods in Natural Language Processing*, pages 1746–1751.

John Lafferty, Andrew McCallum, and Fernando C.N. Pereira. 2001. Conditional Random Fields: Probabilistic Models for Segmenting and Labeling Sequence Data. In *Proceedings of the International Conference on Machine Learning*, pages 282–289.

Guillaume Lample, Miguel Ballesteros, Sandeep Subramanian, Kazuya Kawakami, and Chris Dyer. 2016. Neural Architectures for Named Entity Recognition. In *Proceedings of the 2016 Conference of the North American Chapter of the Association for Computational Linguistics: Human Language Technologies*, pages 260–270.

Donald A.B. Lindberg, Betsy L. Humphreys, and Alexa T. McCray. 1993. The Unified Medical Language System. *Methods of Information in Medicine*, 32(4):281–291.

Yong Luo, Jian Tang, Jun Yan, Chao Xu, and Zhang Chen. 2014. Pre-trained multi-view word embedding using two-side neural network. In *Proceedings on the Twenty-Eighth AAAI Conference on Artificial Intelligence*, pages 1982–1988.

Hongyin Luo, Zhiyuan Liu, Huanbo Luan, and Maosong Sun. 2015. Online Learning of Interpretable Word Embeddings. pages 1687–1692.

Tomas Mikolov, Ilya Sutskever, Kai Chen, Greg Corrado, and Jeffrey Dean. 2013. Distributed Representations of Words and Phrases and their Compositionality. In *Advances in Neural Information Processing Systems*, pages 3111–3119.

Robert Parker, David Graff, Junbo Kong, Ke Chen, and Kazuaki Maeda. 2009. English Gigaword Fourth Edition. *The LDC Corpus Catalog.*, LDC2009T13.

Jeffrey Pennington, Richard Socher, and Christopher D Manning. 2014. GloVe: Global Vectors for Word Representation. In *Proceedings of the 2014 Conference on Empirical Methods in Natural Language Processing*, pages 1532–1543.

Radim Řehůřek and Petr Sojka. 2010. Software Framework for Topic Modelling with Large Corpora. In *Proceedings of the LREC 2010 Workshop on New Challenges for NLP Frameworks*, pages 45–50.

Kirk Roberts and Dina Demner-Fushman. 2016. Interactive use of online health resources: A comparison of consumer and professional questions. *Journal of the American Medical Informatics Association*.

Magnus Sahlgren. 2006. *Vector-Based Semantic Analysis: Representing Word Meanings Based On Random Labels*. Ph.D. thesis, Stockholm University.

Richard Socher, Jeffrey Pennington, Eric Huang, Andrew Y. Ng, and Christopher D. Manning. 2011. Semi-Supervised Recursive Autoencoders for Predicting Sentiment Distributions. In *Proceedings of the 2011 Conference on Empirical Methods in Natural Language Processing*, pages 151–161.

Buzhou Tang, Hongxin Cao, Xiaolong Wang, Qingcai Chen, and Hua Xu. 2014. Evaluating Word Representation Features in Biomedical Named Entity Recognition Tasks. volume 2014, page 240403.

Joseph Turian, Lev Ratinov, and Yoshua Bengio. 2010. Word representations: a simple and general method for semi-supervised learning. In *Proceedings of the 48th Annual Meeting of the Association for Computational Linguistics*, pages 384–394.

Özlem Uzuner, Andreea Bodnari, Shuying Shen, Tyler Forbush, John Pestian, and Brett South. 2011a. Evaluating the state of the art in coreference resolution for electronic medical records. *Journal of the American Medical Informatics Association*, 18:552–556.

Özlem Uzuner, Brett South, Shuying Shen, and Scott L. DuVall. 2011b. 2010 i2b2/VA challenge on concepts, assertions, and relations in clinical text. *Journal of the American Medical Informatics Association*, 18:552–556.

Özlem Uzuner, Anna Rumshisky, and Weiyi Sun. 2013. 2012 i2b2 challenge on temporal relations. *Journal of the American Medical Informatics Association*, (in submission).

Mengqiu Wang and Christopher D. Manning. 2013. Effect of Non-linear Deep Architecture in Sequence Labeling. In *Proceedings of the ICML Workshop on Deep Learning for Audio, Speech and Language Processing*.

Yonghui Wu, Jun Xu, Min Jiang, Yaoyun Zhang, and Hua Xu. 2015. A Study of Neural Word Embeddings for Named Entity Recognition in Clinical Text. In *Proceedings of the AMIA Annual Symposium*, pages 1326–1333.

Wenpeng Yin and Henrich Schütze. 2015. Multichannel Variable-Size Convolution for Sentence Classification. In *Proceedings of the Nineteenth Conference on Natural Language Learning*, pages 204–214.

Ye Zhang and Byron Wallace. 2016. A Sensitivity Analysis of (and Practitioners' Guide to) Convolutional Neural Networks for Sentence Classification. arXiv:1510.03820.

Xiang Zhang, Junbo Zhao, and Yann LeCun. 2015. Character-level Convolutional Networks for Text Classification. In *Advances in Neural Information Processing Systems*, pages 649–657.

Ye Zhang, Stephen Roller, and Byron C. Wallace. 2016. MGNC-CNN: A Simple Approach to Exploiting Multiple Word Embeddings for Sentence Classification. In *Proceedings of the 2016 Conference of the North American Chapter of the Association for Computational Linguistics: Human Language Technologies*, pages 1522–1527.

Jie Zhou and Wei Xu. 2015. End-to-end Learning of Semantic Role Labeling Using Recurrent Neural Networks. In *Proceedings of the 53rd Annual Meeting of the Association for Computational Linguistics*.

Inference of ICD Codes from Japanese Medical Records by Searching Disease Names

Masahito Sakishita
Faculty of Informatics, Shizuoka University,
Japan
msakishita@kanolab.net

Yoshinobu Kano
Faculty of Informatics, Shizuoka University,
Japan
kano@inf.shizuoka.ac.jp

Abstract

Importance of utilizing medical information is getting increased as electronic health records (EHRs) are widely used nowadays. We aim to assign international standardized disease codes, ICD-10, to Japanese textual information in EHRs for users to reuse the information accurately. In this paper, we propose methods to automatically extract diagnosis and to assign ICD codes to Japanese medical records. Due to the lack of available training data, we dare employed rule-based methods rather than machine learning. We observed characteristics of medical records carefully, writing rules to make effective methods by hand. We applied our system to the NTCIR-12 MedNLPDoc shared task data where participants are required to assign ICD-10 codes of possible diagnosis in given EHRs. In this shared task, our system achieved the highest F-measure score among all participants in the most severe evaluation criteria. Through comparison with other approaches, we show that our approach could be a useful milestone for the future development of Japanese medical record processing.

1 Introduction

In these years, more medical institutes adopt EHRs of electronic media replacing paper media. However, natural language processing (NLP) technologies in medical fields tend to be underdeveloped; hospitals and clinics have been extremely reluctant to allow access to clinical data for researchers from outside the associated institutions (Chapman et al., 2011).

In order to develop NLP technologies of medical field, various shared tasks (contests, competitions, challenge evaluations, critical assessments) have been organized. One of the well-known medical-related shared tasks is the Informatics for Integrating Biology and the Bedside (i2b2) by the National Institutes of Health (NIH), which started in 2006 (Uzuner, 2008) now brought in SemEval as Clinical TempEval 2015 (Bethard et al., 2015) and Clinical TempEval 2016 (Bethard et al., 2016). The Text Retrieval Conference (TREC), which addresses more diverse issues, also launched the Medical Reports Track (Voorhees et al., 2012). The first European medical shared task was the ShARe/CLEF eHealth Evaluation Lab (Goeuriot et al., 2015; Kelly et al., 2014; Suominen et al., 2013). While they are mainly targeted at English, medical reports are written in native languages in most countries. Therefore, information retrieval techniques in individual languages are required to be developed.

As a first step of our research for the development of Japanese medical NLP field, we propose methods that automatically extract diagnosis from Japanese EHRs, assigning ICD (International Classification of Diseases) codes[1]. ICD is made by the World Health Organization (WHO) to record, analyze, interpret and compare medical data (disease and cause of death) that has been collected all over the world. The latest version is ICD-10. An ICD code consists of a single letter prefix and numbers (e.g. "I48"). Single letter prefix mostly represents a kind of disease (e.g. "I" stands for *ischemic heart disease*) and numbers represent detailed information of disease (e.g. "I48" stands for "*atrial fibrillation* and *flutter*"). ICD could be used to create machine readable data.

Even a human expert has difficulty assigning an appropriate ICD code. Only doctors with actual clinical experiences could understand real intention of diagnosis. In other words, expert techniques

---

[1] World Health Organization, International Classification of Diseases (ICD), available from :
http://www.who.int/classifications/icd/en/

Proceedings of the Clinical Natural Language Processing Workshop,
pages 64–68, Osaka, Japan, December 11-17 2016.

and experiences are required if a non-professional guesses the intention to assign codes without examining an actual patient. This point makes the automatic ICD coding tasks difficult.

We describe details of our methods in Section 2. Section 3 describes our experiments and results where we applied our system to the shared task data of the NTCIR-12 MedNLPDoc task (Aramaki et al., 2016). Our system achieved the best performance regarding the *Sure* match score of this MedNLPDoc task. Section 4 describes future works of our research and concluding this paper.

2　Method

We suggest five methods that output appropriate ICD code given a Japanese medical record text. In our system, method 2.1 is our base method. We defined methods 2.2-2.4 assuming results of method 2.1. Method 2.5 and part of method 2.4 are independent of method 2.1. We describe our methods one by one below.

2.1　Decision of target sentence

We define a "sentence" as a line of text marked off by the Japanese periodical symbol, "。".

We suggest that there are two types of sentences in medical records: sentences that include diagnosis, and sentences that do not include any diagnosis. The latter type of sentences may include disease names which are not related to any diagnosis.

When a sentence contains diagnosis, and when that sentence contains a name of disease, our system output a corresponding ICD code of that disease name. We describe details of our method below.

We extract sentences that contain a keyphrase to narrow candidate sentences down. For example, the previous example sentence with diagnostic result "検査の結果で慢性化膿性中耳炎と診断され、手術目的に入院となる。(As a result of medical check, diagnosed as *chronic suppurative otitis media*, and hospitalization is needed for an operation.)" has a keyphrase of "と診断され (be diagnosed)" with its diagnosis name of disease before the keyphrase. In addition to the keyphrase "と診断され", we listed and used keyphrases of "の診断 (diagnosis of)" , etc. 30 keyphrases in total. We chose these keyphrases by manually verifying medical records written in Toba (2006) and medical records of MedNLPDoc training data, which details are described later. If a sentence contains a negation, e.g. "認めない (not see)", this sentence is discarded from the candidate sentences.

After selecting sentence candidates, morphological analysis is performed by Kuromoji morphological analyzer[2] with a custom dictionary where Wikipedia entry words and disease names are registered. Disease names are taken from Japanese Standard Disease-Code Master (Hatano et al., 2003). We changed the weight of words in the dictionary in order to make disease names of the dictionary appear preferentially. When a disease name is included in the morphological analysis result, we assign a corresponding ICD code in the table of Japanese Standard Disease-Code Master.

2.2　Translation of medical technical words from English to Japanese

There are many English words used as technical terms in the Japanese medical records, written in alphabets. Because these English words are often not registered in our custom dictionary, we cannot deal with it directly. We used Life Science Dictionary (Ohtake et al., 2008) to translate English words into Japanese words. In this method, we only use dictionary entries which exactly matched with the English words in the medical record.

2.3　Unification of paraphrase words

There are many inconsistent spelling variations appear in the medical records. We deal with this problem by our method below. We use the redirection relations of Wikipedia to make such normalizations, i.e. redirected words correspond to normalized words.

2.4　Assigning ICD codes to disease names including various body parts

In our method described in section 2.1, descriptions like "XX に癌,YY に損傷 (*cancer* of XX,

---

[2] http://www. atilika.org/

damage to YY)" will only output corresponding ICD codes of *damage* or *cancer*, ignoring "XX" and "YY". However, these ignored words could include information required to output appropriate ICD codes. We decided to focus on "*malignant neoplasm*" and "*damage*" in our method. Our system outputs ICD codes from combination of words.

We define rules to detect ICD codes using combination of words that express various parts of body, and the words which represent *malignant neoplasm* and *damage*. We manually made a list of body parts using the Japanese Standard Disease-Code Master.

If a sentence contains both a word of the body parts and a word which represents *malignant neoplasm* or *damage*, our system outputs a corresponding ICD code.

In case of *damage*, we only check sentences selected by our method described in section 2.1, while we used the whole medical record in case of *malignant neoplasm*. This is because there are special keyphrases used for *malignant neoplasm*.

Our system covered almost all ICD codes of "*malignant neoplasm*" and "*damage*", including various body parts. We removed words which represent *malignant neoplasm* or *damage* from the dictionary used in method 2.1, because these words e.g. "癌 (*cancer*):C80" are sometimes used to refer specific concepts e.g. "肺癌 (*lung cancer*):C349" but not for the general meaning.

2.5 Inferring ICD codes from XML tags

We suggest another method that outputs ICD codes using information in XML tags of the MedNLPDoc task dataset. We focused on tags of *anamnesis* (既往歴) and *family clinical history* (家族歴), because there are categories of ICD codes directly correspond to these two types. If there is a tag of *anamnesis* or *family clinical history*, our system outputs an ICD code by extracting clues from words inside these tags. Then we apply the same method described in 2.4 to the extracted words.

3 Experiment and Result

3.1 Experiment Setting

We applied our system to the NTCIR-12 MedNLPDoc task. MedNLP is a shared task series for Japanese medical record texts in NTCIR (NII Testbeds and Community for Information access Research). Previous tasks include three sub tasks: named entity removal task (de-identification task), disease name extraction task (complaint and diagnosis), and normalization task (ICD coding task)(Morita et al., 2013). The MedNLPDoc task is more advanced and practical. In this task, participants' systems infer disease names in ICD. Due to this practical setting, task participants' systems could directly support actual daily clinical services and clinical studies in various areas (Aramaki et al., 2016).

Task organizers created a medical record corpus as a training dataset for this task which includes 200 individual medical records. The average number of sentences per record is 7.82. The average number of codes per record is 3.86. 552 code types appeared in the corpus.

Test dataset consists of 78 clinical texts, which were randomly selected from the past National Examination for Medical Practitioners [3]. Question sentences and graphics were eliminated from the original documents. Then, three professional human coders (more than one-year experience) individually added ICD-10 codes (Aramaki et al., 2016) to the same documents in parallel.

The MedNLPDoc task provides three evaluation metrics. *Sure* metric regards ICD codes which all of three annotators agreed to annotate, *Major* metric for more than two annotators, *Possible* metric

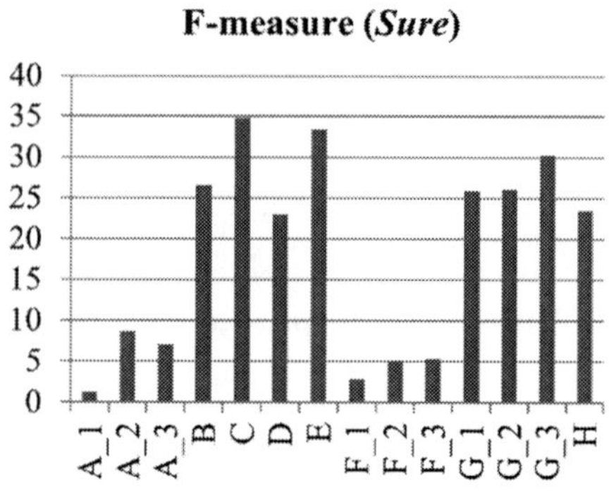

Figure 1. Comparison with other teams in F-measure (*Sure*), where C indicates our result

---

[3] Ministry of Health, Labour and Welfare, Question and the correct answer of the 108th national medical examination, available from : http://www.mhlw.go.jp/seisakunitsuite/bunya/kenkou_iryou/iryou/topics/tp140512-01.html

for more than a single annotator. Because the inter-annotator discrepancy is quite low in this dataset, the *Sure* metric is considered as most reliable.

3.2 Result

We measured our system performance by participating in the MedNLPDoc task. Figure 1 shows results of all participants in the *Sure* evaluation metric. Our result is shown as Team C, which is the best score in F-measure *Sure* metric. Team C is rule-based, while others use machine learning methods, like CRF (Team B, E), CRF and SVM (Team G) (Aramaki et al., 2016).

Combination of Methods	# of system output	# and scores of perfect match				# and scores of 3-digits match			
		#	P	R	F	#	P	R	F
2.1	424	101	23.82	13.08	16.89	161	37.97	20.85	26.92
2.1+2.2	450	110	24.44	14.25	18.00	176	39.11	22.80	28.81
2.1+2.3	479	107	22.34	13.86	17.11	170	35.49	22.02	27.18
2.1+2.4	494	120	24.29	15.54	18.96	208	42.11	26.94	32.86
2.1+2.5	446	111	24.89	14.38	18.23	174	39.01	22.54	28.57
2.1+2.2+2.3+2.4+2.5	597	145	24.29	18.78	21.18	245	41.04	31.74	35.79

Table 1. Evaluation for combinations of methods in Precision (P), Recall (R) and F-measure (F)

3.3 Effect Analysis of Methods

As gold standard annotations of the test dataset are not provided, we conducted another experiment using the training data to show effectiveness of each of our methods. Table 1 shows result of this experiment. "perfect match" means the number of codes perfectly matched with the correct ICD codes. "3-digits match" means the number of output codes which three digits (first letter and next two numbers) are matched. Total number of correct answers was 772. We compared a couple of different combinations of our sub-methods, each described in section 2.1, 2.2, 2.3, 2.4, and 2.5, respectively.

Because the F-measure becomes better when methods 2.2-2.5 are added to 2.1, each individual method can be regarded as effective. When the method 2.4 is added, the growth of F-measure is the largest. Regarding *malignant neoplasms* and *damage*, we can write coding rules easier by hand because corresponding ICD descriptions explicitly discriminates "[body_part] and *damage*", "[body_part] and the *cancer*", etc. Additionally, *malignant neoplasms* and *damage* are frequently appeared in the training data, which made the contribution larger.

When method 2.3 is added, the growth of F-measure is the smallest. Reasons would be that coverage of paraphrases is insufficient with Wikipedia. Another reason is that the training data does not contain many paraphrases.

4 Future work and Conclusion

There should be two criteria required to achieve the ultimate goal of this ICD codes assignment study. The first criterion is whether symptoms are explicitly described or not in medical records. This decision would have almost been achieved by our approach except for *cancers*. Regarding *cancers*, our system could not select candidate sentences effectively in some cases because there were no keyphrases found as other phrases are used. Extracting such indirect expressions would be required.

The second criterion is whether we should output ICD codes or not, when we find out symptom or name of disease. Let us consider *cough* for example, which often appears in medical records. In order for the code of the *cough* to be assigned, we need to know how strong an effect of the *cough* gives to a patient's diagnosis by deriving relationship of the *cough* and main diagnosis. Then we can recognize relationships between symptoms and diagnosis that could contribute to the real clinical works.

If we could properly define these two criteria, we can output more accurate ICD codes.

Japanese medical records contain language specific features like inclusion of diagnosis names, paraphrases, etc. From such features, we made five rule-based methods consisting our system that output ICD codes accurately. Our system performed best among participants in the MedNLPDoc task. However, it is still difficult to output ICD codes perfectly. In order to make better ICD coding in future, it will be required to analyze relationships between a patient's symptom and his/her disease.

References

Aramaki, E., Morita, M., Kano, Y. and Ohkuma, T. (2016). Overview of the NTCIR-12 MedNLPDoc Task, 167–179.

Bethard, S., Derczynski, L., Savova, G., Pustejovsky, J. and Verhagen, M. (2015). SemEval-2015 Task 6: Clinical TempEval. *Proceedings of the 9th International Conference on Semantic Evaluation (SemEval 2015)*, 806–814.

Bethard, S., Savova, G., Chen, W.-T., Derczynski, L., Pustejovsky, J. and Verhagen, M. (2016). SemEval-2016 Task 12: Clinical TempEval. *Proceedings of the 10th International Conference on Semantic Evaluation (SemEval 2016)*, 1052–1062.

Chapman, W. W., Nadkarni, P. M., Hirschman, L., D'Avolio, L. W., Savova, G. K. and Uzuner, O. (2011). Overcoming barriers to NLP for clinical text: the role of shared tasks and the need for additional creative solutions. *Journal of the American Medical Informatics Association : JAMIA*, 18(5), 540–543. doi:10.1136/amiajnl-2011-000465

Goeuriot, L., Kelly, L., Suominen, H., Hanlen, L., Névéol, A., Grouin, C., Palotti, J. and Zuccon, G. (2015). Overview of the CLEF eHealth Evaluation Lab 2015.

Hatano, K. and Kazuhiko Ohe. (2003). Information Retrieval System for Japanese Standard Disease-Code Master Using XML Web Service.

Kelly, L., Goeuriot, L., Schreck, T., Leroy, G., Suominen, H., W.Chapman, W., Martinez, D., Velupillai, S., Mowery, D. L., et al. (2014). Overview of the CLEF eHealth evaluation lab 2014. *Lecture Notes in Computer Science (including subseries Lecture Notes in Artificial Intelligence and Lecture Notes in Bioinformatics)*, 9283, 429–443. doi:10.1007/978-3-319-24027-5_44

Morita, M., Kano, Y., Ohkuma, T., Miyabe, M. and Aramaki, E. (2013). Overview of the NTCIR-10 MedNLP task.

Ohtake, H., Fujita, N., Kaneko, S., Morren, B. and Kawamoto, T. (2008). Anatomy of Life Science English: Lists of common collocates of, (3).

Shibuki, H., Sakamoto, K., Kano, Y., Mitamura, T., Ishioroshi, M., Itakura, K. Y., Wang, D., Mori, T. and Kando, N. (2014). Overview of the NTCIR-11 QA-Lab Task. *the 11th NTCIR (NII Testbeds and Community for information access Research) workshop*, (Task 1), 518–529.

Suominen, H., Salanterä, S., Velupillai, S., W.Chapman, W., Savova, G., Elhadad, N., Pradhan, S., South, B. R., Mowery, D. L., et al. (2013). Overview of the CLEF eHealth Evaluation Lab 2013, 1–20.

Toba, K. (2006). *ICD Coding Training(Second edition) in Japanese*. Igakushoin.

Uzuner, O. (2008). Second i2b2 workshop on natural language processing challenges for clinical records. *AMIA Annual Symposium proceedings*, 1252–1253.

Voorhees, E. M. and Hersh, W. (2012). Overview of the TREC 2012 Medical Records Track. *The Twentieth Text REtrieval Conference*.

A fine-grained corpus annotation schema of German nephrology records

Roland Roller[*], **Hans Uszkoreit**[*], **Feiyu Xu**[*], **Laura Seiffe**[*], **Michael Mikhailov**[*◇],
Oliver Staeck[◇], **Klemens Budde**[◇], **Fabian Halleck**[◇] and **Danilo Schmidt**[◇]
[*]Language Technology Lab, DFKI, Berlin, Germany
{firstname.surname}@dfki.de
[◇]Charité Universitätsmedizin, Berlin, Germany
{firstname.surname}@charite.de

Abstract

In this work we present a fine-grained annotation schema to detect named entities in German clinical data of chronically ill patients with kidney diseases. The annotation schema is driven by the needs of our clinical partners and the linguistic aspects of German language. In order to generate annotations within a short period, the work also presents a semi-automatic annotation which uses additional sources of knowledge such as UMLS, to pre-annotate concepts in advance. The presented schema will be used to apply novel techniques from natural language processing and machine learning to support doctors treating their patients by improved information access from unstructured German texts.

1 Introduction

Long-term treatment and follow-up of chronically ill patients result in complex medical data and patient records. Although such data is nowadays to a large extent digitalized in various hospital information systems or clinical databases, information is mostly unstructured and difficult to access. Thus, reliable methods to access useful information in clinical data would clearly support physicians. An information extraction system could be applied in the clinical routine to analyze individual patient records for alarming symptoms, historical events, contraindications or side effects. Furthermore it could help to identify subgroups of patients with special characteristics, identify patients for clinical studies or correlating medication and symptoms in historical patient data. Automated information extraction could allow the development of alert systems, which help the clinicians in their daily routine and thus would increase patients safety. However, the first step towards any information extraction is the definition of information of interest, such as diseases, medications or dosing size. This information is then defined within an annotation schema and is used to manually annotate a gold standard corpus to train and evaluate information extraction methods.

Unfortunately, manual annotation is time consuming (Kim et al., 2008) and expensive (Angeli et al., 2014). In particular in the medical domain, expert knowledge is often required which makes the annotation process even more difficult and costly. Therefore existing schemata and corpora could be used in order to save time and effort for the annotation of new data. On the other hand, existing schemata might not cover the information of interest. Furthermore, most of the existing and assessable clinical data sets are in English language. The existing German-language clinical data sets are not freely available. Consequently, we aim to create a new gold standard corpus for German data. This work introduces an annotation schema for reports of the nephrology domain which is based on the requirements of physicians in our project and is motivated by linguistic aspects of German language. The schema takes into account that current German medical dictionaries (which often support named entity recognition) are much smaller than the English ones. Hence, we include annotations on a fine-grained level, in particular in the context of compound words. Moreover, the annotation process includes an automatic pre-annotation step to decrease the duration of manual annotation and to generally ease the annotation process (Batista-Navarro et al., 2015; Kwon et al., 2014).

The paper is structured as follows: The next section presents related work. An overview of relevant data sources is provided in Section 3. The following Section 4 introduces the annotation schema with a

Proceedings of the Clinical Natural Language Processing Workshop,
pages 69–77, Osaka, Japan, December 11-17 2016.

range of different examples. The semi-automatic annotation process is reported in Section 5. The paper finishes with results and future work.

2   Related Work

Information extraction from clinical data has become an important research topic in recent years. With the increasing amount of medical data (such as clinical notes or discharge summaries), the development of reliable text analytics tools could support physicians to better access patient data. However, annotated data sets are required for the development and testing of information extraction methods. Most of the existing annotated clinical data sets are in English language. There are only a few data sets that have been created for non-English languages, such as for Swedish (Skeppstedt et al., 2014), French (Névéol et al., 2015) or Polish (Mykowiecka et al., 2009). For German, only a few sources and clinical corpora exist and will be introduced in the following.

The two most relevant sources for this work are described in Bretschneider et al. (2013) and Toepfer et al. (2015). Bretschneider et al. (2013) focused on the classification of sentences in radiology reports as either pathological and non-pathological based on the given findings. Toepfer et al. (2015) addressed the extraction of fine-grained information from German transthoracic echocardiography reports. The presented terminology involves three main types: objects, attributes and values. Unfortunately, both data sets are not publicly available.

Another very interesting corpus is the FraMed corpus which is described in Wermter and Hahn (2004). The authors present a German-language medical text corpus containing manually supplied sentence boundary, token segmentation and part-of-speech (POS) tags. Due to the fact that the corpus cannot be legally accessed by a third party, Faessler et al. (2014) present an freely available tool for segmentation and POS tagging for German clinical data, based on models trained on the FraMed corpus. Further relevant sources for German clinical data are for instance the German Specialist Lexicon (Weske-Heck et al., 2002) or the German MeSH[1]. A good overview is also provided in the work of Schulz et al. (2013).

3   Utilized Data Sources

This section presents the two data sources used for this work. Firstly, a biomedical knowledge source is presented which is used to automatically pre-annotate data to reduce annotation time. Secondly, the textual data which is used for the annotation is introduced and then analyzed by its (linguistic) characteristics.

3.1   UMLS

The Unified Medical Language System[2] (UMLS) is a large biomedical knowledge base containing millions of medical terms and relations between them. The core component, the Metathesaurus, unifies more than 120 biomedical knowledge vocabularies, such as the Medical Subject Heading (MeSH), the Medical Dictionary for Regulatory Activities (MedDRA) or the International Classification of Diseases, Tenth Revision, Clinical Modification (ICD-10-CM).

Medical concepts can be described in different ways with different spellings, different abbreviations and also in different languages. UMLS unifies those variations using the Concept Unique Identifier (CUI). Furthermore, UMLS links each CUI against at least one semantic type, such as 'Finding', 'Sign or Symptom' for instance. Most of the concepts are defined in English. However, more than 200,000 German entries can be found[3] in UMLS.

In this work, UMLS will be used for two different purposes. First of all, German concepts of the Metathesaurus are used to pre-annotate data by aligning semantic types to concepts of our annotation schema (see Section 5). Furthermore, unique CUIs should be assigned to annotated concepts in our corpus (normalization against UMLS) at a later stage. Normalization helps to access data more efficiently. Rather than searching for the string *'Niereninsuffizienz'* (*'renal insufficiency'*) we can use its

---

[1] http://www.dimdi.de/static/en/klassi/mesh_umls/mesh/index.htm
[2] https://www.nlm.nih.gov/research/umls/
[3] UMLS 2016AA, including all German sources

UMLS-CUI *C1565489* which includes different variations in German, such as '*Insuffizienz der Niere*', '*beeinträchtigte Nierenfunktion*' or '*Nierenfunktionsbeeinträchtigung*'.

3.2 Clinical text of the nephrology domain

The annotation task in this paper is conducted within the MACSS[4] (Medical Allround-Care Service Solutions) project, which focuses on improving the safety of patients after kidney transplantation. A key focus of this project is to improve the communication with the patient via a mobile app and to facilitate data exchange and bilateral communication between physicians. Another important goal of this project is the improvement of drug safety by analysis of potentially dangerous drug-drug interactions. In this context the text annotation aims to generate a corpus for the detection of correlated information in historical patient data (e.g. by correlating medication and symptoms). In addition, we want to analyze individual patient records in order to identify alarming symptoms, contraindications or side effects of medications.

At the current project stage German discharge summaries and clinical notes of a hospital's kidney transplant department are annotated. The content of the data set has two peculiar characteristics compared to clinical data of other domains: First, the topic in the documents is related to kidney transplant patients and second, the patients are under a long-term treatment. Both types of documents (discharge summaries and clinical notes) are generally written by medical doctors and have significant differences. The clinical notes are rather short and are written by doctors during or shortly after a visit of a patient. The currently used documents consider only those sections which are addressed to other physicians outside the hospital, such as family doctors or the physician who transferred the patient.

	Discharge Summaries	Clinical Notes
#documents available	118	1607
#words (total)	89691	68480
#sentences (total)	16068	11871
avg. words per document (std. deviation)	760.09 (208.62)	42.61 (35.74)

Table 1: Comparison of our Clinical Data Sources

Discharge summaries instead are written during a stay at the hospital. The document is more structured. It contains information about medical history, diagnosis, condition, medication etc. of the patient. Discharge summaries contain much more text compared to clinical notes and are often written by physicians. Furthermore, discharge summaries often contain longer and more well-formed sentences.

Table 1 provides a brief analysis of both document types. Discharge summaries contain a larger average number of words per document compared to the clinical notes[5]. However, the standard deviation of the avgerage word number per document shows that both document types have a large variation in text length. Some clinical notes contain only a few words.

3.2.1 Data Characteristics

The clinical data of this project share the same characteristics as other clinical documents across the world, such as syntactic shortened and reduced semantic complexity. Additionally, the texts contain a large number of Greek- and Latin-rooted words. Often, only keywords are used, together with a lot of abbreviations which are not entirely consistently used over the different texts/authors (Kim et al., 2011). Spelling mistakes and indirect colloquial patient language ('patient reports that legs were tickling') might occur. Besides, texts vary concerning writing style and information density. Due to the nature of German language the documents are also rich in inflection forms and compounds.

Overall, especially linguistic characteristics are of great interest defining our annotation schema: we assume that linguistic resources play a major role in the understanding of the structure of medical data.

---

[4]`http://macss-projekt.de/`

[5]The information is generated by applying a German tokenizer and a sentence splitter. All non alphabetical tokens are removed.

The German language tends to have a complex sentence- and word structure. While the former varies a lot between different texts and is therefore hard to generalize, the latter is worthy to be considered in more detail.

First of all, characteristics of part-of-speeches (POS) and word formation processes like derivation and composition seem to be important for a deeper understanding. Beside nouns also adjectives and verbs support detailed textual information as presented in Example 1. The example shows, that crucial information can be also expressed by an adjective (1a) or a verb (1b).

(1)   a. [Depressive] Episode ('depressive episode')
       b. Wir übernahmen den Patienten [intubiert] ('we took over an intubated patient')

In German the POS of a word can be easily changed by derivation processes (Fleischer, 2012) which means, that given concepts are not limited to a specific word category. For this reason it is necessary to not solely rely on the POS distribution and to keep concepts open to various POS. Example 2 illustrates the described situation. 'Delirant' and 'im Delirium', both mean that the patient is in an acute confusional state ('delirium'). While the former is grammatically used as (predicative) adjective, the latter is used as noun.

(2)   a. Der Patient war [delirant] ('the patient was delirous')
       b. Der Patient war im [Delirium] ('the patient had delirium')

The same situation applies to changes from noun to verb (or vice versa):

(3)   a. Es erfolgte die [Sedierung] ('sedation was undertaken')
       b. Wir [sedierten] den Patienten ('we sedated the patient')

Compounds like those presented in Example 4 are a very typical phenomenon of the German language and work really productive: They can be built by nearly every POS, yet compounds can be formed by other compounds. This grammar device is frequently used in our corpus.

(4)   a. Niereninsuffizienz ('Renal insufficiency')
       b. Aortenklappenstenose ('Aortic valve stenosis')

'Niereninsuffizienz' can be paraphrased as 'Insuffizienz der Niere' (literally: 'insufficiency of the kidney'). The given example shows that a fine-grained examination of lexemes help gaining more information than a simple review of the surface does. In Example 4a, a body part in combination with a medical condition might span a new and more specific medical condition, whereas the body part expresses the location of the condition.

4   Annotation Schema

For this work information related to the patient, the disease pattern and the treatment are of interest. In order to answer these superordinate questions, relevant concepts are created that structure the information supporting entities: therefore, focus is on the elements that express medical conditions, their treatments, and further diagnostic procedures. Consequently, the concepts 'Medical_Condition', 'Treatment', and 'Diagnostic/Lab_Procedure' are the most important and the most frequent ones. However, also other concepts, such as 'Body_Part' or 'Medication' for instance are important information and considered for the annotation.

Besides further information such as time and location, negations/speculations and some structural data is of interest. Thus, all those elements often serve as specification of the preceding concepts. The development of the concepts took place by manually examining example corpora.

Table 2 presents the list of entities we currently annotate. The relevant entities are grouped into different categories such as *time information* or *person/body*. Furthermore the table provides a brief explanation of each entity. Note, *Biomedical_Chemistry* is currently grouped into the category *therapy*. However, depending on the context the concept can also occur in the category *Person/Body*.

Category	Entity	Explanation
Time Information	Date	Point in time; date
	Temporal_Course	Temporal courses; other temporal information
Person/Body	Person	Mentions of individuals
	Body_Part	Body parts; organs
	Tissue	Body's own tissues
	Body_Fluids	Body's own fluids
	Local_specification	Anatomical descriptions of position and direction
Process	Process	Body's own biological processes
Condition	State_of_Health	Positive, wanted finding; contrary to *Medical_Condition*
	Medical_Condition	Symptom, Diagnosis and observation
	Diagnostic/Lab_Procedure	All types of tests used to diagnose a disease or to assess the patients' state
	Medical_Specification	Closer definition; describing lexemes, often adjectives
	Degree	State of degrees, e.g. degree of a tumor disease
	Type	Closer definition/specification
Therapy	Medical_Device	Medical devices, utilities and material
	Medication	Drugs, medicine
	Biological_Chemistry	Biochemical substances
	Treatment	Therapeutic procedures, treatments
	Measurement	Measurements and the corresponding units
Structure	Structure_Element	Text structuring elements
Truth	Modality_Positive	Explicitly positive lexeme
	Modality_Negation	Negation particle
	Modality_Vagueness	Vagueness expressing elements

Table 2: Relevant concepts

Medical_Condition comprises a wide range of entities. In fact, entities describing findings, diseases and syndromes are all covered by that single concept. Even professionals cannot always distinguish for certain between a disease and a symptom, for instance in case of hypertension. Hypertension can be categorized as a disease or as a symptom, e.g. of a chronic renal insufficiency. By normalizing concepts to UMLS, a distinction can be achieved in later working steps, if required.

As mentioned above, the development of the concepts does not base on the lexeme's grammatical structure (e.g. the POS) but on its semantic value. Thus, also other aspects of the surface structure may vary: the concept *temporal_course* can occur as a word strings (5a), as a scheme for the dosing of medication (5b), or as an prefix within a lexeme (5c).

(5)   a. [Seit drei Tagen] ('For three days')

        c. Urbason 4 mg [1 - 0 - 0 - 0] ('Urbason 4 mg 1 - 0 - 0 - 0')

        b. [Post]extubationem ('after the extubation')

As illustrated in Section 3.2.1, concepts like *Medical_Condition* are not limited to a certain POS. Conversely, there are some exceptions which appear exclusively in adjectival form: *Medical_Specification* and *Local_Specification* occur only in describing, thus in adjectival position. They do not contain the main information (the patient's medical condition and treatments) but serve as further specification. The concept *State_of_Health* is also a special case regarding its POS-structure. Due to its contrary meaning to *Medical_Condition* it might be assumed, that it occurs within the same position and same context. However, *State_of_Health* is actually only used as adjective. Similar to that, the concept *Type* occurs only in one certain position, namely as the first constituent of a compound, see Example 6:

(6)   a. [Druck]schmerz ('tenderness and/or pain on palpation')

While most of the concepts base on their semantic value, *Structure_Element* is an exception because its use does not rely on its meaning but on its function. These entities occur as kind of headlines that structure the texts. Additional information throughout the paragraph can be gained by accentuating these elements. Further examples are given in Table 3.

Examples (German; English)	Annotation
Sonographie der **Leber** (Ultrasound examination of the **liver**)	Body_part
Ovarialzyste (**ovarial** cyst)	Body_part
inhomogenem NiGEN**parenchym** (inhomogeneous renal **parenchyma**)	Tissue
laterales Weichteilrelease (**lateral** soft tissue release)	Local_specification
Sonographie der **linken** Niere (ultrasound examination of the **left** kidney)	Local_specification
Reaktion auf Licht (**Reaction** to light)	Process
physiologische Darm**geräusche** (physiologic bowel **sounds**)	Process
Haut **warm** und **trocken** (skin **warm** and **dry**)	State_of_Health
terminale NiGEN**insuffizienz** (terminal renal **insufficiency**)	Medical_Condition
EKG vom 24.01.2000 (**ECG** from 24.01.2000)	Diagnostic/Lab_Procedure
Röntgen Thorax in zwei Ebenen (chest **radiography** in two projections)	Diagnostic/Lab_Procedure
chronische NTx-Glomerulonephritis (**Chronic** glomerulonephritis of the renal allograft)	Medical_Specification
Transplantatversagen nach chronischer NTx-Glomerulonephritis (Renal **allograft** failure after chronic glomerulonephritis of the renal allograft)	Medical_Device
chronische Niereninsuffizienz **Stadium III** (Chronic kidney disease **stage 3**)	Degree
Primärimplantation (**primary** implantation)	Type
Transaminasenanstieg (Elevation of **transaminases**)	Biological_Chemistry
Wir übernahmen den Patienten **sediert**, **intubiert** und **beatmet** (We took over the **sedated**, **intubated** and mechanically **ventilated** patient.)	Treatment
Nephrektomie (Nephrectomy)	Treatment
Tumorausdehnung beträgt **4,5 x 3 x 6 cm**. (Tumor dimensions are **4,5 x 3 x 6 cm**)	Measurement
keine Ödeme (**no** oedemas)	Modality_Negative

Table 3: Annotation Schema - Concept Examples

4.1 Annotation Process

The annotation process aims at a detailed annotation level. This means, that the annotation attempts to detect many information in the documents, but also to consider a fine-granularity. The following example in Figure 1 motivates the granularity. The term 'terminale Niereninsuffizienz' ('terminal renal insufficiency') will be annotated on different levels:

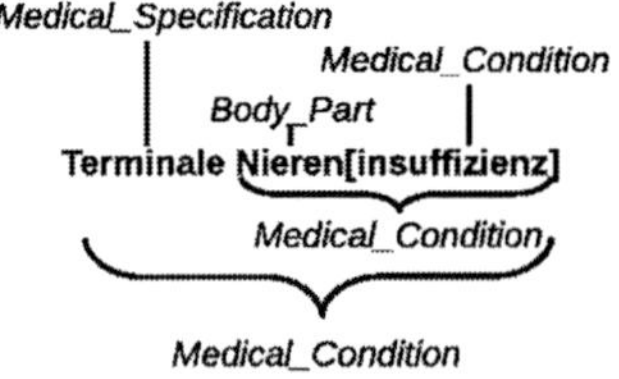

Figure 1: Annotation Granularity

First of all the complete term 'terminale Niereninsuffizienz' will be annotated as *medical_condition*, which is closest to the UMLS entry. Besides also 'Niereninsuffizienz' and 'insuffizienz' will be annotated as *Medical_Condition* in order to achieve a fine-granularity. Furthermore strings such as 'terminale' ('terminal') will be annotated as *Medical_Specification* and 'Niere' ('renal/kidney') as *Body_Part*.

There are different reasons for the detailed annotation level. Firstly, 'terminale Niereninsuffizienz' is the most specific term which includes all other information. Often NER systems target the longest and most specific match. However, UMLS might not cover necessarily all variants. Even more problematic is the fact, that medical terms of interest might be not covered by the German subset of UMLS. A fine granularity might help at a later stage to learn larger constructs (e.g. adjective + compound noun) which are not in the dictionary.

The fine-granularity can be carried to extremes: Some *Local_Specifications* provide special information due to derivation processes, see Example 7:

(7) intrapulmonal ('intrapulmonary')

The first constituent of the lexeme, 'intra-' comes from a finite set of Latin-rooted prefixes which name directional and locational information. 'Pulmonal' is also a Latin-rooted element which can be translated as 'concerning the lungs' ('pulmo' is Latin for 'lung' and the suffix '-al' indicates an adjective). In combination with the prefix 'intra', which means 'inside sth.', the lexeme's meaning is 'inside the lungs' what would be annotated as *Local_Specification*. Since UMLS has no entry for the German lexeme, this fine-grained analysis can provide a deeper understanding.

5 Semi-Automatic Annotation

The annotation is carried out by three students: two linguists, which are familiar with the domain and one medical expert. The medical student is responsible to annotate data and to support the other two students. The annotation task is conducted using the Brat[6] annotator tool. As seen in (Batista-Navarro et al., 2015) or (Kwon et al., 2014), an automatic pre-annotation can help to decrease the duration of manual annotation and to generally ease the annotation process. For this reason an automatic annotation step will be also included into this annotation. In the following the automatic pre-annotation and the preliminary manual annotation will be described.

5.1 Pre-Annotation

To decrease the duration of manual annotation and to generally ease the annotation process, the corpus is pre-annotated automatically[7] beforehand. In this way, falsely tagged elements can be easily corrected and missing annotations included.

The pre-annotation reads in the text documents and applies a tokenization. Currently up to four tokens are considered and matched to the German and English subset of UMLS. Furthermore also substring matches are allowed in order to detect the different components of compound words. The pre-annotation can be divided into three parts: regex, dictionary-lookup and UMLS dictionary lookup. Concepts which are less likely to be found in UMLS are covered by the first two steps. This information usually describes descriptive information of main concepts.

The regex annotation covers the concepts *Measurement*, *Date*, *Temporal_Course*, and *Structure_Element*. Whereas the first three concepts include numbers, in combination with some measurements or month, such as 'mg', 'ml' or 'January', the concept *Structure_Element* detects text spans followed by a colon (':'). These structuring elements usually define the topic of the following text or section and can be used to build up relations to the concepts found in the follow-up text.

The dictionary lookup considers words which are less likely to be found in UMLS as single concepts. Many of the concepts considered here are used to further specify concepts such as *Body_Part* or *Medical_Condition*. In German, many of those concepts (in particular *Medical_Specification* and *Local_Specification*) occur as adjectives or adverbs. In contrast to our approach, UMLS assigns those specifications directly into the surrounding concept, such as 'akute Blutungsanaemie' ('acute haemorrhagic anaemia') or 'papilläres Schilddrüsenkarzinom' ('papillary thyroid carcinoma') and not necessarily as a single concept. This dictionary is manually generated.

word	substring
'Empfehlungen' ('suggestions')	'Lunge' ('lung')
'Behandlung' ('Treatment')	'Hand' ('hand')

Table 4: Substring Matching Errors

The UMLS dictionary lookup searches within a window of 4 tokens for German, stemmed German and English words in UMLS. In order to avoid additional errors only capitalized words are considered for English. This pre-annotation component bases on aligning semantic types of UMLS to concepts of our annotation schema. The mapping schema is presented in Table 5. It means, that if a mention can be found in UMLS, its semantic type is examined and if the type matches to one of our concepts, the

---

[6] http://brat.nlplab.org/
[7] The tool will be made available here: http://macss.dfki.de

Concept name	STY-Name
Person	Human; Patient or Disabled Group
Body_Part	Body Part, Organ, or Organ Component; Body Location or Region
Tissue	Tissue
Body_Fluids	Body Substance
Local_Specification	Spatial Concept
Process	Biologic Function; Physiologic Function; Organism Function; Mental Process; Organ or Tissue Function; Cell Function
State_of_Health	Qualitative Concept
Medical_Condition	Anatomical Abnormality; Congenital Abnormality; Acquired Abnormality; Finding; Sign or Symptom; Pathologic Function; Disease or Syndrome; Mental or Behavioral Dysfunction; Neoplastic Process; Injury or Poisoning
Diagnostic/Lab_Procedure	Laboratory Procedure; Diagnostic Procedure
Medical_Specification	Organism Attribute; Clinical Attribute; Qualitative Concept
Medical_Device	Medical Device
Medication	Clinical Drug; Pharmacologic Substance; Antibiotic
Biological_Chemistry	Biomedical or Dental Material; Biologically Active Substance; Hormone; Enzyme; Vitamin; Immunologic Factor; Receptor; Organic Chemical; Nucleic Acid, Nucleoside, or Nucleotide; Amino Acid, Peptide, or Protein; Inorganic Chemical; Element, Ion, or Isotope; Gene or Genome
Treatment	Therapeutic or Preventive Procedure
Measurement	Quantitative Concepts

Table 5: Mapping Semantic Types to our Annotation Schema

string will be pre-annotated. Additionally the annotation will be extended by its definitions (if defined in UMLS) and its source vocabularies.

The substring matcher also relies on the UMLS dictionary lookup and searches for tokens longer than 3 characters in the German sources. The substring matcher produces various errors as seen in Table 4. However, during the annotation process models and exceptions will be updated to improve the pre-annotation gradually.

Another component of the annotation is an additional synonym dictionary. During the annotation process newly annotated and frequently occurring concepts should be examined in more detail. In this case annotators search for synonyms or English translations in order to find a corresponding entry in UMLS and to extend the German UMLS dictionary.

5.2 Current Annotation Process

At the current stage of the annotation, many files are annotated by at least two different annotators. Annotation differences are then discussed together in a group in order to find the best solution and to ensure a mutual understanding of the annotation task. Using the new annotations the pre-annotation can be successively improved by including new knowledge and addressing frequent errors (such as described in Table 4).

6 Results and Future Work

In this work we presented a fine-grained annotation schema for German clinical text, used for the domain of nephrology. The schema is motivated by linguistic aspects and addresses the needs of clinicians and medical professionals in our project. Furthermore we presented a semi-automatic annotation process in order to ease the annotation procedure. After finishing the concept annotations, the corpus will be normalized against UMLS and extended by relations. The corpus serves as baseline for further information access of patient data in a hospitals' transplant center.

Acknowledgements

This research was supported by the German Federal Ministry of Economics and Energy (BMWi) through the project MACSS (01MD16011F).

References

Gabor Angeli, Julie Tibshirani, Jean Wu, and Christopher D. Manning. 2014. Combining Distant and Partial Supervision for Relation Extraction. In *Proceedings of the 2014 Conference on Empirical Methods in Natural Language Processing (EMNLP)*, Doha, Qatar. Association for Computational Linguistics.

Riza Batista-Navarro, Jacob Carter, and Sophia Ananiadou. 2015. Semi-automatic curation of chronic obstructive pulmonary disease phenotypes using argo. In *Proceedings of the Fifth BioCreative Challenge Evaluation Workshop*, pages 403–408.

Claudia Bretschneider, Sonja Zillner, and Matthias Hammon. 2013. Identifying pathological findings in german radiology reports using a syntacto-semantic parsing approach. In *Proceedings of the 2013 Workshop on Biomedical Natural Language Processing*, pages 27–35, Sofia, Bulgaria, August. Association for Computational Linguistics.

Erik Faessler, Johannes Hellrich, and Udo Hahn. 2014. Disclose models, hide the data - how to make use of confidential corpora without seeing sensitive raw data. In Nicoletta Calzolari (Conference Chair), Khalid Choukri, Thierry Declerck, Hrafn Loftsson, Bente Maegaard, Joseph Mariani, Asuncion Moreno, Jan Odijk, and Stelios Piperidis, editors, *Proceedings of the Ninth International Conference on Language Resources and Evaluation (LREC'14)*, Reykjavik, Iceland, may. European Language Resources Association (ELRA).

Wolfgang Fleischer. 2012. *Wortbildung der deutschen Gegenwartssprache*. Walter de Gruyter.

Jin-Dong Kim, Tomoko Ohta, and Jun'ichi Tsujii. 2008. Corpus annotation for mining biomedical events from literature. *BMC Bioinformatics*, 9(1).

Youngjun Kim, John Hurdle, and Stphane M Meystre. 2011. Using UMLS lexical resources to disambiguate abbreviations in clinical text. *Annual Symposium proceedings*, 2011:715–722.

Dongseop Kwon, Sun Kim, Soo-Yong Shin, Andrew Chatr-aryamontri, and W. John Wilbur. 2014. Assisting manual literature curation for proteinprotein interactions using bioqrator. *Database*, 2014.

Agnieszka Mykowiecka, Małgorzata Marciniak, and Anna Kupść. 2009. Rule-based information extraction from patients clinical data. *Journal of Biomedical Informatics*, 42(5):923 – 936. Biomedical Natural Language Processing.

Aurélie Névéol, Cyril Grouin, Xavier Tannier, Thierry Hamon, Liadh Kelly, Lorraine Goeuriot, and Pierre Zweigenbaum. 2015. CLEF ehealth evaluation lab 2015 task 1b: Clinical named entity recognition. In *Working Notes of CLEF 2015 - Conference and Labs of the Evaluation forum, Toulouse, France, September 8-11, 2015*.

Stefan Schulz, Josef Ingenerf, Sylvia Thun, and Philipp Daumke. 2013. German-language content in biomedical vocabularies. In *Working Notes for CLEF 2013 Conference , Valencia, Spain, September 23-26, 2013*.

Maria Skeppstedt, Maria Kvist, Gunnar H. Nilsson, and Hercules Dalianis. 2014. Automatic recognition of disorders, findings, pharmaceuticals and body structures from clinical text: An annotation and machine learning study. *Journal of Biomedical Informatics*, 49:148 – 158.

Martin Toepfer, Hamo Corovic, Georg Fette, Peter Klügl, Stefan Störk, and Frank Puppe. 2015. Fine-grained information extraction from german transthoracic echocardiography reports. *BMC Medical Informatics and Decision Making*, 15(1):1–16.

Joachim Wermter and Udo Hahn. 2004. An annotated german-language medical text corpus. In *Proceedings of the Forth International Conference on Language Resources and Evaluation*, Lisbon, Portugal.

Gesa Weske-Heck, Albrecht Zaiss, Matthias Zabel, Stefan Schulz, Wolfgang Giere, Michael Schopen, and Rüdiger Klar. 2002. The german specialist lexicon. *Proceedings AMIA Annual Symposium*, pages 884–888.

Detecting Japanese Patients with Alzheimer's Disease based on

Word Category Frequencies

Daisaku SHIBATA, Shoko WAKAMIYA, Eiji ARAMAKI
Nara Institute of Science and Technology (NAIST)
8916–5 Takayama, Ikoma City, 630–0192, Japan
`{shibatadaisaku.rr8,wakamiya,aramaki}@is.naist.jp`

Ayae KINOSHITA
Kyoto University Graduate School of Medicine
Syogoin, Sakyo-ku, Kyoto City, 606–8507, Japan
`kinoshita.ayae.6v@kyoto-u.ac.jp`

Abstract

In recent years, detecting Alzheimer's disease (AD) in early stages based on natural language processing (NLP) has drawn much attention. To date, vocabulary size, grammatical complexity, and fluency have been studied using NLP metrics. However, the content analysis of AD narratives is still unreachable for NLP. This study investigates features of the words that AD patients use in their spoken language. After recruiting 18 examinees of 53–90 years old (mean: 76.89), they were divided into two groups based on Mini Mental State Examination (MMSE) scores. The AD group comprised 9 examinees with scores of 21 or lower. The healthy control group comprised 9 examinees with scores of 22 or higher. Linguistic Inquiry and Word Count (LIWC). The word frequency was found from observation. Significant differences were confirmed for the usage of impersonal pronouns in the AD group. This result demonstrated the basic feasibility of the proposed NLP-based Alzheimer's disease detection approach.

1   Introduction

The increasing life expectancy has led to severe health and social problems. Among them, the most severe problem is the rising frequency of Alzheimer's disease (AD; Wortmann 2015) among the population. Japan is especially faced with a crisis posed by AD. Japan's Ministry of Health, Labour and Welfare reported that more than 1 in 4 control individuals would soon be afflicted with mild cognitive impairment (MCI) or AD. If all afflicted people were treated for MCI and AD, then the cost is estimated to be as high as 10 trillion dollars per year. As the number of patients with AD increases, the needs of these individuals might eventually exceed the current capacity of the national healthcare system, requiring various methods to detect the early stages of AD, prevent further deterioration, and alleviate requirements for care. Natural language processing (NLP) has also drawn much attention as a novel and simple method to detect AD using language.

Roark et al. indicated that a spoken narrative recall task can discriminate between healthy control people and those with MCI (Roark, Mitchell et al. 2011). Tanaka et al. proposed a computer avatar based approach to detect dementia in very early stages (Tanaka et al. 2016). Aramaki et al. also specifically examined the patients' narratives during a test (Aramaki et al. 2016). Year by year, MCI and AD narratives have been newly analyzed using NLP.

Although the details of the methods differ among them, they share the same approach, examining functional features (such as audio and transcript of narrative recall task by Roark et al.), spoken dialog by Tanaka et al. and transcriptions written and spoken narratives and vocabulary size by Aramaki et

Proceedings of the Clinical Natural Language Processing Workshop,
pages 78–85, Osaka, Japan, December 11-17 2016.

al.) (Aramaki et al. 2016)) to detect and characterize patients with a disease. They did not deal with the contents of the narratives. In contrast, this paper presents a new method to detect AD based the categories of words patients use in spoken narratives. The word categories are classified by Linguistic Inquiry and Word Count (LIWC), a dictionary for text analysis.

To date, it has generally been pointed out that words from people with AD differ from those of healthy control people, including slowed speech, word-finding hesitation, sentences with abnormal words, and using words that are mispronounced or incomprehensible[1]. Especially, it is often said that AD patients more frequently use pronouns (e.g. it, that) than healthy control people. An example is presented in Figure 1. The sample includes much silence, repeating similar utterances, and pronouns.

Using the LIWC, this study empirically investigates the proportion of word categories between AD and healthy control people. Our review of the literature indicates that this report is the first quantitative study investigating the word categories associated with AD in Japanese. The statistics is presented in Table 1.

> Ummm, ummm, what were those?
> ... Oh no.
> Well, they were all food, weren't they?
> A plant?
> A plant... a plant... was *it* a cherry blossom?
>
> (Omitted)
>
> What were the *other* 2? There was a pencil, a watch and what else? ... I cannot remember *it*. Ah, well, a key. And there was, there was a pencil here. And that one. What was the 3rd one here? ...... There was a key. ...... There was a key and I cannot remember the next one. ... I don't know. What was *it*? Tell me.

Figure 1: Speech of a patient with AD in Mini-Mental State Examination (MMSE score) (Translated into Japanese). *Italic* indicates personal impersonal pronouns.

Maximum	1569
Minimum	242
Median	688
Average	788

Table1: Word Statistics in Corpus.

Contributions of this study can be summarized as shown below.
- A LIWC analysis is conducted for narratives uttered by people suspected of having AD.
- This study also examines a proposed method for LIWC translation.

2   Related Work

Recent studies of early detection methods such as blood testing and detailed memory testing have revealed vast improvements in detection capabilities (Mapstone et al. 2014). However, most of these methods are physically or mentally invasive, which has led to anticipation of less-invasive or even non-invasive detection methods. Dementia symptoms include degenerative cognitive decline, as well as behavioral and functional disorders. The disease also results in the deterioration of various executive functions, reasoning, and language abilities. Among these, language deficits have been shown to be more apparent from the early stages of dementia (Snowdon et al. 1996). These deficits include naming disorders, auditory and written comprehension impairment, fluent but empty speech, and semantic paraphasia. However, repetition capabilities and articulation are often preserved (Appell et al. 1982). Reportedly, the impairment of language abilities in dementia patients is often inconsistent because semantic and pragmatic language abilities are likely to become more impaired, whereas syntax and phonology demonstrate better preservation (Schwartz et al. 1979). Semantic errors reportedly are

---

[1] http://www.businessinsider.com/changes-in-president-reagans-speech-early-sign-of-alzheimers-2015-4

the most common and distinct language deficit because dementia patients tend to substitute target names with superordinate category names or demonstrate circumlocutory speech with impaired naming (Emery 2000). Other reports have also described unrelated errors (Moreaud et al. 2001), phonological errors (Croot et al. 2000), and visual errors (Croot et al. 2000). However, these are often dependent on the type of picture confrontation naming task, the severity or stage of the disease, or other unique patient-level circumstances (Geda 2012). MCI, part of which constitutes a pre-stage of dementia, might indicate a boundary between aging-related non-dementia reduction in cognition and dementia on the spectrum of cognitive function.

Using the above characteristics, various dementia screening methods have been proposed to date. Table 2 shows the summary of previous screening studies. Well-known studies were those conducted by Roark et al. (Roark et al. 2007; Roark et al. 2011), which analyzed the lexical features and syntactic feature from transcripts of spoken narrative such as neuropsychological approaches (Moriyama et al. 2015) and automatic speech analysis approaches (König et al. 2015). Some of them used automatic speech recognition (Tóth et al. 2015). Aramaki et al. specifically examined vocabulary size in speech transcription (Aramaki et al. 2016). Tanaka et al. proposed a novel approach using computer avatars (Tanaka et al. 2016). In addition Orimaye et al. (Orimaye et al. 2014) used machine learning algorithms to build diagnostic models using syntactic and lexical features and Jarrold et al. used LIWC for aided diagnosis of Dementia (Jarrold et al. 2014).

Author	Method	Disease	Sample size	Year
Aramaki et al. (Aramaki et al. 2016)	Analysis of vocabulary size in speech	MCI, AD	22	2016
Tanaka et al. (Tanaka et al. 2016)	Spoken dialog with computer avatars	MCI	18	2016
König et al. (König et al. 2015)	Automatic speech analyse	MCI, AD	64	2015
Tóth et al. (Tóth et al. 2015)	Acoustic indicator	MCI	51	2015
Moriyama et al. (Moriyama et al. 2015)	Neuropsychological battery	AD	299	2015
Orimaye et al. (Orimaye et al. 2014)	Machine learning algorithms	AD	556	2014
Jarrold et al. (Jarrold et al. 2014)	Analysis of spontaneous speech	AD	48	2014
Roark et al. (Roark et al. 2011)	Transcript with audio	MCI	74	2011
Roark et al. (Roark et al. 2007)	Lexical features and syntactic features	MCI	55	2007

Table 2: Earlier studies.

3   Materials

We have collected narratives of hospital patients to build the corpus.

3.1   Research field

Criteria used for the experiment are the following.
[Inclusion criterion]

- **AD group (AD)**: Patients with Alzheimer's disease between light MCI and middle class MCI (MMSE below 21 points).
- **Healthy control group (HC)**: Patients without AD. Healthy control people group members are age-matched with AD group members (MMSE over 22 points)[2].

[Exclusion criteria]

- Patients who have some other brain-related diseases
- Non-native Japanese speakers

We recorded conversations between a patient and a medical staff member using an IC recorder. Then, we transcribed the conversations manually. Table 3 presents characteristics of the patients.

---

[2] Healthy control people might actually have diseases (other than AD).

Age	Sex	MMSE
72	Woman	4
71	Woman	14
90	Woman	17
80	Man	18
73	Woman	19
78	Woman	19
81	Woman	20
73	Man	21
77	Woman	21

(a) AD

Age	Sex	MMSE
77	Man	22
81	Woman	22
72	Woman	22
87	Man	25
53	Man	25
87	Woman	26
82	Woman	26
79	Man	28
71	Woman	30

(b) HD

Table 3: Participant attributes.

3.2 Ethics Statement

The experiment is explained to patients (or their family). If they cannot understand the explanation, then we exclude them. We do not reward the patients. The use of these data for research purposes was approved by the ethics committee of Kyoto University (approval NO. E2525).

3.3 MMSE – based Patient Classification

The goal of this study is to detect important features that can classify AD and others by analyzing their spoken narratives. Thus, we determine a person is AD or not (MCI and normal) based on Mini Mental State Examination (MMSE). The MMSE is a simple inspection method for a subject suspected as AD. In this test, a patient is asked 11 questions; their answers are judged by the score (max 30; min 0). The MMSE scores between 30 and 27 points are normal; those between 26 and 22 points might be MCI; and those below 21 points might be AD.

4 Language Resource LIWC

4.1 What is LIWC

We use Linguistic Inquiry and Word Count (LIWC) as a language resource for classifying words into corresponding categories. LIWC has been developed by researchers who are interested in social, clinical, health, and cognitive psychology. We can classify people's social and psychological states using LIWC. However because LIWC is only for English, it is difficult to apply to Japanese texts. Our review of literature indicates that no resource for Japanese is comparable with LIWC.

Therefore, we make Japanese LIWC by translating English LIWC. We arrange categories for Japanese LIWC by considering a gap depending on the language differences. Table 4 shows 64 categories in English LIWC. Then we extract 22 categories related to diseases by the judgment of the authors, as shown in Table 5. We remove categories that are not related to our target disease (e.g. <Body>). We also remove categories that are not translatable to Japanese. (e.g. <Article>).

<Funct>	<Ipron>	<Sad>	<Incl>	<Adverbs>	<Family>	<Body>	<Work>
<Pronoun>	<Article>	<CogMech>	<Excl>	<Prep>	<Friends>	<Health>	<Achiev>
<Ppron>	<Verbs>	<Insight>	<Percept>	<Conj>	<Humans>	<Sexual>	<Leisure>
<I>	<AuxVb>	<Cause>	<See>	<Negate>	<Affect>	<Ingest>	<Home>
<We>	<Past>	<Discrep>	<Hear>	<Quant>	<Posemo>	<Relativ>	<Money>
<You>	<Present>	<Tentat>	<Feel>	<Numbers>	<Negemo>	<Motion>	<Relig>
<SheHe>	<Future>	<Certain>	<Bio>	<Swear>	<Anx>	<Space>	<Death>
<They>	<Filler>	<Inhib>	<Nonflu>	<Social>	<Anger>	<Time>	<Assent>

Table 4: English LIWC categories. (64 categories)

<Time>	<Posemo>	<Ipron>	<Sad>	<Family>	<Negemo>	<Present>	<Humans>
<Future>	<Space>	<Anger>	<Negate>	<SheHe>	<I>	<Friends>	
<Social>	<Past>	<Verbs>	<We>	<Anx>	<They>	<You>	

Table 5: Disease - related categories. (22 categories)

4.2 LIWC Translation Procedure

We translate LIWC into Japanese to produce Japanese LIWC as shown below.
- **Step 1**: All words in English LIWC were translated using EDICT (an electric dictionary produced by EDP and JimBreen[3]).
- **Step 2:** One worker searched mistakenly translated words by sight and deleted them. As a result, 5,534 words out of 6,211 words remained.
- **Step 3**: If a duplicated pairs of a Japanese word and its category are found, then we put them together such that 4,769 words out of 5,534 words remained.
- **Step 4**: When conducting morphological analysis for Japanese, we ignore words in the category <Past>. Then the words of verbs belonging to the category <Present> is changed to <Verbs>. We remove three categories <We>, <SheHe>, and <They> and words belonging to these because it was determined that these categories have no correlation with disease.

    Therefore, the number of categories are reduced from 22 to 19.
- **Step 5**: Words in multiple categories are assigned to the most appropriate category by one worker. In Japanese, it is difficult to distinguish between words related to <Time> and those related to <Space>. Therefore, we define a new category called <TimeSpace>. The number of categories becomes 20. We apply these steps to 2,700 words.

5 Experiments

5.1 Procedure

We analyze the corpus as explained below.
- **Step 1**: Texts are analyzed morphologically and stemmed using a Japanese morphological analyzer (Kurohashi and Nagao 2003).
- **Step 2**: The results are consulted by Japanese LIWC. We then count the LIWC word in the corpus.
- **Step 3**: We investigate the ratio of LIWC word frequency for each category.

5.2 Results

The results of t-test are presented in Table 6. In order to the examine the difference between speech of AD group and HC group in a statistical manner. Note that we investigated the difference of the average values in AD and HC group. As shown in Table 6, no significant difference was found between AD and HC in any categories, except for four: <Social>, impersonal pronoun <Ipron>, anxiety <Anx>, <Verbs>, and <Present>. As for <Anx>, HC's value is 0. Figure 2 presents results of the category frequency of AD and HC.

Category	AD (avg.)	HC (avg.)	*p-value*	Difference
<Ipron>	**0.0385**	**0.0268**	**0.0187**	0.0117
<Anx>	0.0008	0	0.0192	0.0008
<Verbs>	**0.0524**	**0.043**	**0.0219**	0.0094
<Present>	**0.0171**	**0.0103**	**0.0226**	0.0068
<Social>	**0.0063**	**0.0116**	**0.0229**	-0.0053
<I>	0.004	0.0019	0.0591	0.0021
<Space>	0.017	0.0231	0.0893	-0.0061
<Posemo>	0.006	0.0076	0.1245	-0.0016
<Time>	0.0364	0.0418	0.1433	-0.0054
<Sad>	0	0.0002	0.1733	-0.0002
<You>	0.0003	0.0002	0.2687	0.0001
<Family>	0.0015	0.0021	0.3135	-0.0006
<Negate>	0.0397	0.0464	0.3264	-0.0067
<Negemo>	0.0006	0.0009	0.3294	-0.0003
<Anger>	0.0004	0.0006	0.3392	-0.0002
<Humans>	0.0068	0.0077	0.3432	-0.0009
<Friends>	0.0008	0.0006	0.4019	0.0002
<Past>	0.0003	0.0003	0.4909	0
<Future>	0	0	-	0
<TimeSpace>	0	0	-	0

Table 6: Values that has significant differences between AD and HC (p-value < 0.05) are **under lined**.

---

[3] http://www.edrdg.org/jmdict/edict.html

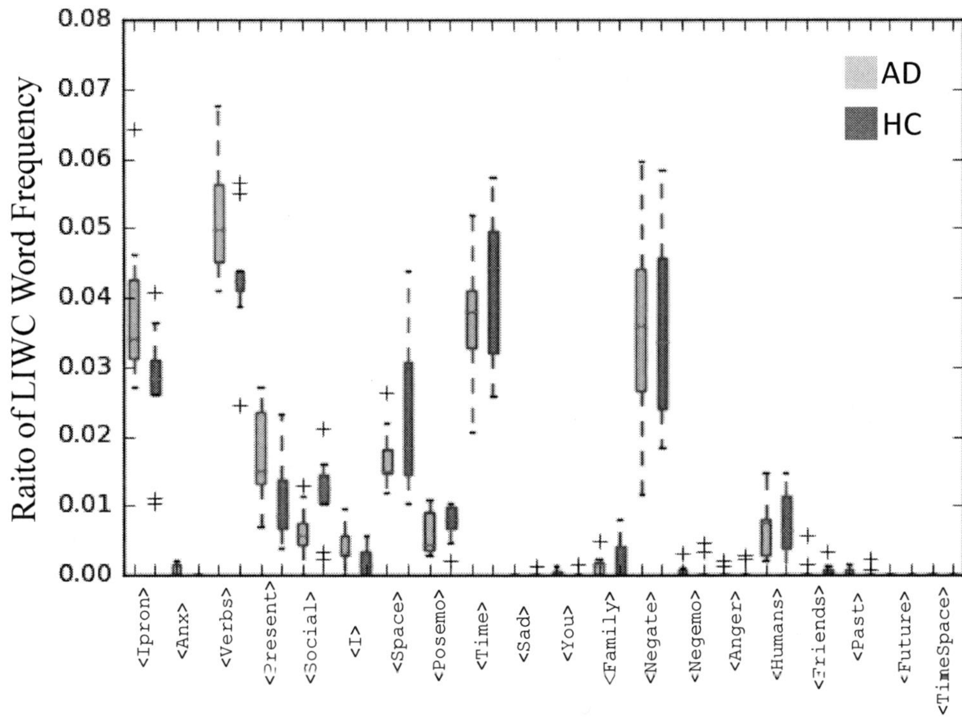

Figure 2: Category frequency of AD (green) and HC (red). Significant differences were found for <Ipron>, <Anx>, <Verbs>, <Present>, and <Social>.

6 Discussion

First, we discuss the findings based on quantitative evidence obtained from a previous study (Sec. 6.1). Then we examine the results by using machine learning (Sec. 6.2).

6.1 Findings: Quantitative Evidence of Previous Study

We discuss categories for which significant differences between AD and HC are observed. The values of <Social> in AD group were significantly lower than those in HC group. Generally, it is said that participating in social activities is effective to prevent AD progression. In other words, a person with little social contact tends to develop AD. Consequently, this result corresponds with AD features. The values of <Ipron> in AD group were significantly higher than those in HC group. AD patients become forgetful. Therefore, they use many impersonal pronouns (Almor et al. 1999). Viewed from a grammatical perspective, ellipses of a subject or objects of a verb are not allowed. They often appear as a pronoun in English, but the ellipsis of them is allowed in the Japanese language. Considering this feature, it is possible that the use of impersonal pronouns becomes more frequent in the condition of AD, particularly for Japanese speakers. Similarly, it corresponds with general AD features. The values of <Verbs> and <Present> in AD group were also significantly larger than those in HC group. However, it is difficult to understand why these results were obtained. Therefore, in future work, it will be necessary to investigate the words in these categories in detail.

Consequently, some observed results supported the previous findings on AD. Although most of the previous studies have been based on subjective observations, our findings provide quantitative evidence for their claims, demonstrating the effectiveness of our approach.

6.2 Decision Tree

In order to the most important clue to classify patients into AD and HC, a decision tree is constructed as shown in Figure 3. It has feature values representing probabilities to be classified into AD or HC in categories.

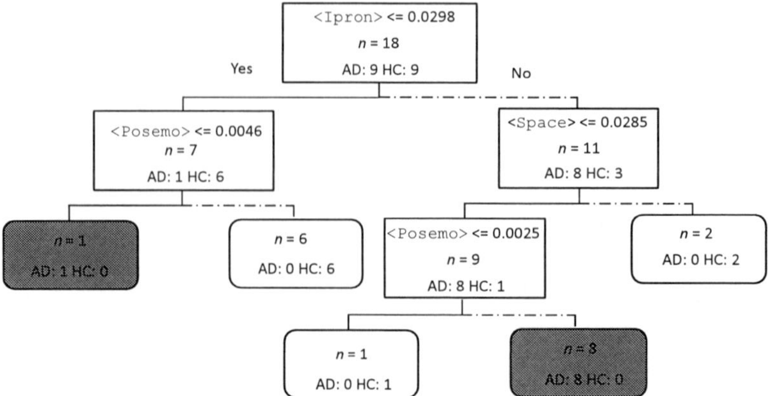

Figure 3: Decision tree results for AD screening.

Figure 3 shows that there are two cases for a person to be diagnosed as AD. The first case is that of using words in <Ipron> below 0.0298 and the value using words in <Posemo> below 0.0046. The probability is 100% to be classified into AD. The other case is that the percentage of impersonal pronouns <Ipron> is higher than 0.0298, the percentage of Space <Space> is less than 0.0285 and the percentage of Positive emotion <Posemo> is higher than 0.0025. The probability is also 100% for classification into AD. Results demonstrate that the values of appearance of words of <Ipron>, <Space> and <Posemo> in conversation are important for AD screening.

7 Conclusion

This study investigated features of the words that AD patients used in their utterances. 18 examinees of 53–90 years old (mean: 76.89) were recruited and divided into two groups based on their MMSE scores. Linguistic Inquiry and Word Count (LIWC) classified words were used to categorize the words that the examinees used. Then their frequency was ascertained. This report is the first of a quantitative study that investigated the word categories of AD. Significant differences were found for the AD group in the usage of several LIWC categories, including impersonal pronouns, which suggests that this simple method can be used for dementia screening.

References

Appell, J., A. Kertesz and M. Fisman (1982). "A study of language functioning in Alzheimer patients." *Brain and Language* 17(1): 73-91.

Aramaki, E., S. Shikata, M. Miyabe and A. Kinoshita (2016). "Vocabulary Size in Speech May Be an Early Indicator of Cognitive Impairment." *PLoS One* 11(5): e0155195.

Croot, K., J. R. Hodges, J. Xuereb and K. Patterson (2000). "Phonological and articulatory impairment in Alzheimer's disease: a case series." *Brain and Language* 75(2): 277-309.

Emery, V. O. B. (2000). "Language impairment in dementia of the Alzheimer type: a hierarchical decline?" *The International Journal of Psychiatry in Medicine* 30(2): 145-164.

Geda, Y. E. (2012). "Mild cognitive impairment in older adults." *Current Psychiatry Reports* 14(4): 320-327.

König, A., A. Satt, A. Sorin, R. Hoory, O. Toledo-Ronen, A. Derreumaux, V. Manera, F. Verhey, P. Aalten and P. H. Robert (2015). "Automatic speech analysis for the assessment of patients with predementia and Alzheimer's disease." *Alzheimer's & Dementia: Diagnosis, Assessment & Disease Monitoring* 1(1): 112-124.

Kurohashi, S. and M. Nagao (2003). Improvements of Japanese Morphological Analyzer JUMAN. Treebanks, *Springer*.

Mapstone, M., A. K. Cheema, M. S. Fiandaca, X. Zhong, T. R. Mhyre, L. H. MacArthur, W. J. Hall, S. G. Fisher, D. R. Peterson and J. M. Haley (2014). "Plasma phospholipids identify antecedent memory impairment in older adults." *Nature Medicine* 20(4): 415-418.

Moreaud, O., D. David, A. Charnallet and J. Pellat (2001). "Are semantic errors actually semantic?: Evidence from Alzheimer's disease." *Brain and Language* 77(2): 176-186.

Moriyama, Y., A. Yoshino, K. Yamanaka, M. Kato, T. Muramatsu and M. Mimura (2015). "The Japanese version of the Rapid Dementia Screening Test is effective compared to the clock-drawing test for detecting patients with mild Alzheimer's disease." *Psychogeriatrics*.

Orimaye, S. O., J. S.-M. Wong and K. J. Golden (2014). Learning predictive linguistic features for Alzheimer's disease and related dementias using verbal utterances. *Proceedings of the First Workshop on Computational Linguistics and Clinical Psychology (CLPsych)*.

Roark, B., M. Mitchell and K. Hollingshead (2007). Syntactic complexity measures for detecting mild cognitive impairment. *Proceedings of the Workshop on BioNLP 2007: Biological, Translational, and Clinical Language Processing*, Association for Computational Linguistics.

Roark, B., M. Mitchell, J. P. Hosom, K. Hollingshead and J. Kaye (2011). "Spoken Language Derived Measures for Detecting Mild Cognitive Impairment." *IEEE Trans Audio Speech Lang Process* 19(7): 2081-2090.

Schwartz, M. F., O. S. Marin and E. M. Saffran (1979). "Dissociations of language function in dementia: A case study." *Brain and Language* 7(3): 277-306.

Snowdon, D. A., S. J. Kemper, J. A. Mortimer, L. H. Greiner, D. R. Wekstein and W. R. Markesbery (1996). "Linguistic ability in early life and cognitive function and Alzheimer's disease in late life: findings from the Nun Study." *JAMA* 275(7): 528-532.

Tanaka, H., H. Adachi, N. Ukita, T. Kudo and N. Satoshi (2016). Automatic Detection of Very Early Stage of Dementia through Spoken Dialog with Computer Avatars. *IEEE Engineering in Medicine and Biology Society*.

Tóth, L., G. Gosztolya, V. Vincze, I. Hoffmann and G. Szatlóczki (2015). Automatic detection of mild cognitive impairment from spontaneous speech using ASR, *ISCA*.

Wortmann, M. (2015). World Alzheimer report 2014: Dementia and risk reduction. Alzheimer's & Dementia: *The Journal of the Alzheimer's Association* 11(7): P837.

Jarrold, W., Peintner, B., Wilkins, D., Vergryi, D., Richey, C., Gorno-Tempini, M. L., & Ogar, J. (2014). Aided diagnosis of dementia type through computer-based analysis of spontaneous speech. In *Proceedings of the ACL Workshop on Computational Linguistics and Clinical Psychology* : pages 27-36.

Almor, A., Kempler, D., MacDonald, M. C., Andersen, E. S., & Tyler, L. K. (1999). Why do Alzheimer patients have difficulty with pronouns? Working memory, semantics, and reference in comprehension and production in Alzheimer's disease. *Brain and language*, *67*(3), 202-227.

Prediction of Key Patient Outcome from Sentence and Word of Medical Text Records

Takanori Yamashita[1], Yoshifumi Wakata[1], Hidehisa Soejima[2], Naoki Nakashima[1],
Sachio Hirokawa[3]

[1]Medical Information Center, Kyushu University Hospital, Fukuoka, Japan
[2]Saiseikai Kumamoto Hospital, Kumamoto, Japan
[3]Research Institute for Information Technology, Kyushu University, Fukuoka, Japan
{t-yama, wakata, nnaoki}@med.kyushu-u.ac.jp
hidehisa-soejima@saiseikaikumamoto.jp, hirokawa@cc.kyushu-u.ac.jp

Abstract

The number of unstructured medical records kept in hospital information systems is increasing. The conditions of patients are formulated as outcomes in clinical pathway. A variance of an outcome describes deviations from standards of care like a patient's bad condition. The present paper applied text mining to extract feature words and phrases of the variance from admission records. We report the cases the variances of "pain control" and "no neuropathy worsening" in cerebral infarction.

1 Introduction

1.1 background

Many medical institutes have been accumulating large amounts of medical data. Medical data include structured numerical data and unstructured text data. Unstructured text data is a wide variety of expressions. However, those data are essential, since those free texts are written by medical staff who actually take care of the patients. Therefore, analyzing medical text is expected to improve medical process and the clinical decision support (Meystre, 2008; Zhua, 2013).

There is previous text mining research on medical records. (Mowery, 2012) applied SVM (Support Vector Machine) to partition the emergency reports into SOAP (Weed, 1969) segments. The prediction of the disease or a cancer classification to the discharge summaries was studied in (Suzuki, 2008; Nguyen, 2010). (Coden, 2009) construct the model that automatically populates pertinent parts of a structured cancer representation from text pathology reports. These are mainly classification and performance evaluation. On the other hand, there are not many contents to which specific sentence and word appeared the symptom and the condition are provided.

1.2 Clinical pathway

A clinical pathway determines standard medical procedures for an inpatient with respect to each disease and to each medical treatment. This is also expected to improve medical management by advancing standardization. The Japanese Society for Clinical Pathway[1] promotes the construction of a standard electronic clinical pathway aiming at the standardization of medical treatment and improvement in medical processes.

"All variance outcome oriented clinical pathway" is a series of medical treatment units which consist of three layers of (a) outcome, (b) assessment and (c) task (Figure 1). Doctors or nurses in medical practice keep records of their tasks and assessments of patients' conditions. The variance is recorded in an outcome layer when a patient's condition doesn't achieve the criteria of an assessment layer. Thus, we can grasp abnormal condition of the patient and the change of medical intervention plan (Nakashima, 2007).

The present paper applied text mining and machine learning to admission records to extract the words that represent outcome variance (patient condition) and evaluated the prediction performance. Furthermore, we considered the patient condition related to the outcome variance from extracted feature words and sentences.

---

[1]http://www.jscp.gr.jp

Proceedings of the Clinical Natural Language Processing Workshop,
pages 86–90, Osaka, Japan, December 11-17 2016.

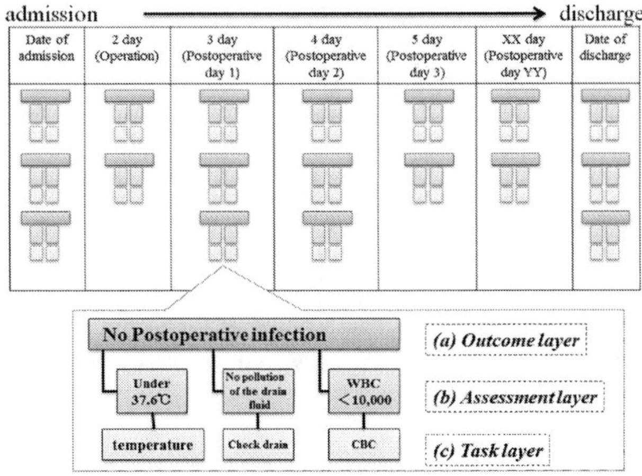

Figure 1: The 3-layer structure of Clinical Pathways

2 Data and Method

2.1 Admission Text Records

In this paper, we analyzed the admission records of 1,222 patients to whom clinical pathway of cerebral infarction was applied in Kumamoto-Saiseikai Hospital in April 2014 – January 2016.

The clinical pathway of cerebral infarction has set 14 outcomes (Table 1). "no paralysis" and "no depressed level of consciousness" cover the large part of variances. However, we focus in the present paper on "pain control" and "no neuropathy worsening", since they are considered clinically important. In order to analyze the 1,222 admission records, we constructed a search engine of the textual records. We used GETA[2] system available at NII GETA project. Using this search engine, we tried extraction of the words that may serve as a determinant of outcome variance.

Outcome	Variance count
no Paralysis	1026
no depressed level of Consciousness	734
Dietary intake	522
Vital stable	513
Pain control *	456
no Neuropathy worsening *	356
Circulatory dynamics stable	157
no Urination disorder	133
Respiratory status stable	122
no Chest Infection symptom	14
no Side effect symptom	12
keep Rest	6
no Dyscoria symptom	4
no Imbalance syndrome symptom	1

Table 1: Outcome in clinical pathway of Cerebral Infarction (*: target in this study)

2.2 Classification by Support Vector Machine and Feature Selection

We applied SVM to predict if an admission record is in the outcome variance. The specific procedure is as follows. All admission records are vectorized after morphological analysis using medical dictionary

---

[2]http://geta.ex.nii.ac.jp/geta.html

(about 80,000 words). If a patient's record contains the outcome, it is labeled as positive example. In contrast, the cases which have no mark are used as negative data. Then the classification model is constructed using SVM (SVM-light (Joachims, 1999)).

we applied the model to the imaginary sentence that consists of a single word wi. We used the predicted score of the sentence as the score(wi) of the word.

The $score(w_i)$ denotes the SVM score of a word w_i obtained by applying the model to the imaginary document that contains only the word. In (Sakai, 2012), the $score(w_i)$ was used for the feature selection. In the present paper, we propose another two measures to evaluate the importance of each word. The first measure $score(w_i) * df(w_i)$ is obtained as the product of the document frequency $df(w_i)$ of the word. The second measure $log(score(w_i) * df(w_i))$ is product of the log of the document frequency of the word and the score. Those measures are defined as "w.o, d.o, l.o". Furthermore, the measure for which the absolute value was used "w.a, d.a, l.a" was established and 6 measures were used because there was also score of negative in SVM.

Then, we applied the model to all sentences to evaluate the score of each sentences. The top scored sentences were chosen as typical sentences of the outcome variance. We highlighted the feature words in those sentences to help interpreting the meaning of the sentence with focused feature words.

3 Result

3.1 Feature Words and Feature Sentences

Table 2 lists the top 30 positive words as feature words for the outcomes of "pain" and "neuropathy worsening". Table 2 shows feature sentences that contain such feature words. There are many sentences of "pain" that contain "dizzy", "headache", "nausea", "fibroid" and "aneurysm". The sentences of "neuropathy worsening" often shows "paralysis", "right face" and "difficulty talking".

Outcome	Feature words	Feature setences
Pain	dizzy(132), hypalgesia(14), aneurysm(181)*, headache(81)*, nifedipine(67), nausea(61), fibroid(27), right angular(53), calcification(68), pravastatin(23), hemianopsia(94)	dizzy when body move, severe nausea. Feeling badness, a headache and dizziness appear suddenly. found aneurysm in cavernous sinus. anamnesis: fibroid, gallstone(postoperation), high blood pressure, irregular pulse.
Neuropathy worsening	paralysis(205), right face(106), renal failure(60), right knee(10), hypalgesia(14), sick sinus syndrome(15), Right facial paralysis(88), difficulty talking(165), flexion(65)*	When getting up, the paralysis of a right hand finger appeared and was also felt by the right face again. With the paralysis senses in mandibular nerve area of right face. The paralysis sense of the right face, the right forearm and the right thigh back side. Difficulty talking appeared. Forgetfulness and slow talking appeared.

Table 2: Feature words and sentences by SVM (* possibility or impossibility, presence or absence)

3.2 Feature Selection

The top N of positive words and negative words (or the top 2N of the absolute value) were selected to construct a model, and then we evaluated the prediction performance. We varied the number of words N (N=1,2,···,10,20,···, 100,200,···). We used 5-fold cross validation in the evaluation experiment. The prediction performance was evaluated by Accuracy and F-measure.

The baseline Accuracy of "pain" that uses all words is 0.58. The Accuracy is obtained 0.64 at N=9 (l.o, l.a), and then the best of Accuracy is attained 0.77 at N=700 (w.o, w.a) as shown in Figure 2. The baseline F-measure of "pain" that uses all words is 0.39. The F-measure is obtained 0.55 at N=30, and is attained 0.65 at N=100 (w.o, w.a) and 0.81 at N=700 (w.o, w.a) as shown in Figure 3.

The baseline Accuracy of "neuropathy worsening" that uses all words is 0.61. The Accuracy obtained 0.70 at N=3 (d.o, d.a) and around 0.75 at N=100 (6 measures), and then is attained 0.85 at N=700 (w.o, w.a) as shown in Figure 4. The baseline F-measure of "neuropathy worsening" that uses all words is 0.33. The best of F-measure is attained 0.60 at N=100 (w.o) and 0.75 at N=700 (w.o, w.a) as shown in Figure 5. The measure of Score and Score*Df made high performance.

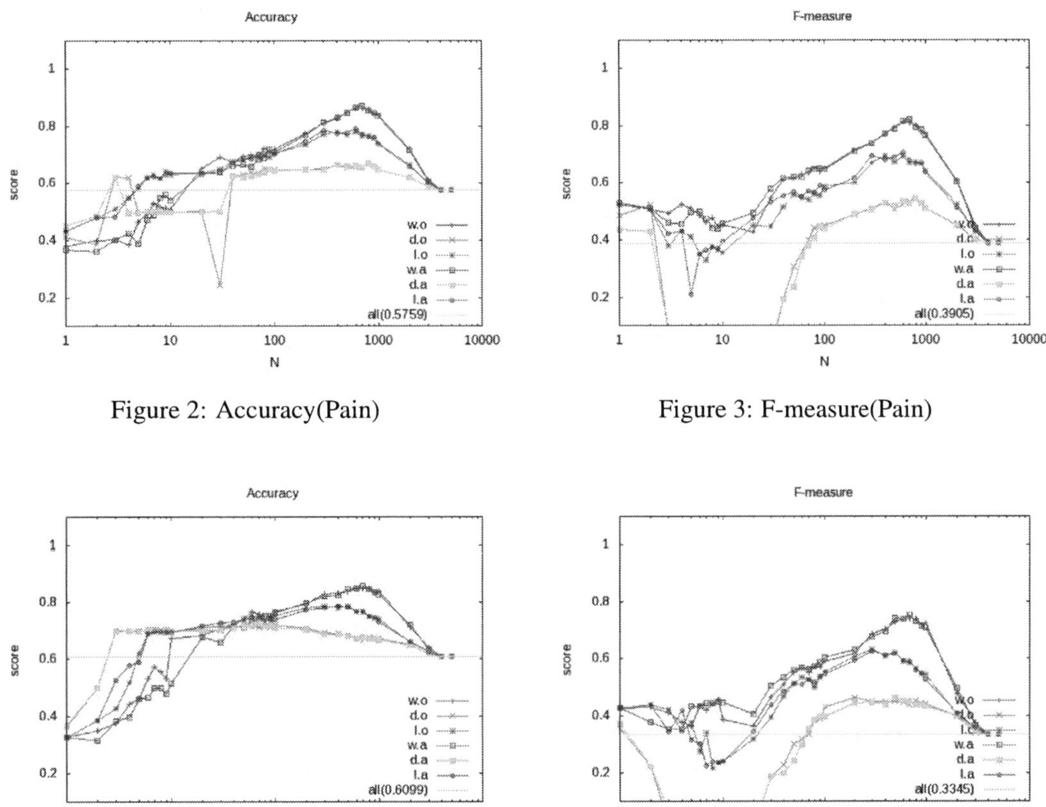

Figure 2: Accuracy(Pain)

Figure 3: F-measure(Pain)

Figure 4: Accuracy(Neuropathy worsening)

Figure 5: F-measure(Neuropathy worsening)

4   Conclusion

This present paper reported the extraction of feature words and typical sentences that describe the patient condition from the free texts. "dizzy", "headache" and "nausea" are extracted as feature words of "pain". "paralysis", "difficulty talking" and "right face" are extracted as feature words of "neuropathy worsening". These words make sense from a clinical viewpoint. Furthermore, the Accuracy with less than 10 words was better for the prediction performance than F-measure with it by feature selection in both the cases.

In the present paper, we considered feature sentences that contain those feature word and then interpreted context of the sentence. As the result, we succeeded in extracting the part of the patient's site and the typical condition of the patient from feature words and feature sentences. Then, it will enable early care to critical indicator. We plan to analyze other outcomes and other cases. We aim to establish a method of medical text mining that can perform clinical evaluation for the improvement medical processes.

Acknowledgements

This research is partially supported by JSPS KAKENHI Grand Number 15H02778

References

Meystre SM. Savova GK. Kipper-Schuler KC and Hurdle JF. 2008. *Extracting information from textual documents in the electronic health record: a review of recent research* Yearbook of medical informatics, 128–144.

Zhua F. Patumcharoenpolc P. Zhanga C. Yanga Y. Chang J. Meechai A. Vongsangnak W and Shen B. 2013. *Biomedical text mining and its applications in cancer research* Journal of Biomedical Informatics, 46(2):200–211.

Nakashima N. Okada H. and Gouchi A. 2007. *Hospital Information System and Clinical Pathways* Japan journal of medical informatics, 27(1):21–28 (in Japanese).

Sakai T. and Hirokawa S. 2012. *Feature Words that Classify Problem Sentence in Scientific Article* Proceedings of the 14th International Conference on Information Integration and Web-based Applications & Services, 360–367.

Yamashita T. Wakata Y. Hamai S. Nakashima Y. Iwamoto Y. Flanagan B. Nakashima N and Hirokawa S. 2015. *Presumption Model for Postoperative Hospital Days from Operation Records* International Journal of Computer & Information Science, 1(16):50–59.

Mowery D. Wiebe J. Visweswaran S. Harkema H and Chapman WW 2012. *Building an automated SOAP classifier for emergency department reports* Journal of Biomedical Informatics, 45(1):71–81.

Suzuki T. Yokoi H. Fujita S and Takabayashi K 2008. *Automatic DPC code selection from electronic medical records: Text mining trial of discharge summary* Methods of Information in Medicine, 47(6):541–548.

Nguyen AN. Lawley MJ. Hansen DP. Bowman RV. Clarke BE. Duhig EE and Colquist S 2010. *Symbolic rule-based classification of lung cancer stages from free-text pathology reports* Journal of the American Medical Informatics Association, 17(4):440–445.

Coden A. Savova G. Sominsky I. Tanenblatt M. Masanz J. Schuler K. Cooper J. Guan W and de Groen PC 2009. *Automatically extracting cancer disease characteristics from pathology reports into a Disease Knowledge Representation Model* Journal of Biomedical informatics, 42(5):937–949.

Weed LL 1969. *Medical Records, Medical Education, and Patient Care. Cleaveland* Western Reserve University

Joachims T, 1999. *Making large-scale support vector machine learning practical* Advances in kernel methods,169–184

Unsupervised Abbreviation Detection in Clinical Narratives

Markus Kreuzthaler[a,b]
[a]CBmed GmbH
Center for Biomarker Research in Medicine
Stiftingtalstrasse 5, 8010 Graz, Austria

Michel Oleynik[b], Alexander Avian[b] and **Stefan Schulz[b]**
[b]Institute for Medical Informatics, Statistics and Documentation
Medical University of Graz
Auenbruggerplatz 2, 8036 Graz, Austria

Abstract

Clinical narratives in electronic health record systems are a rich resource of patient-based information. They constitute an ongoing challenge for natural language processing, due to their high compactness and abundance of short forms. German medical texts exhibit numerous ad-hoc abbreviations that terminate with a period character. The disambiguation of period characters is therefore an important task for sentence and abbreviation detection. This task is addressed by a combination of co-occurrence information of word types with trailing period characters, a large domain dictionary, and a simple rule engine, thus merging statistical and dictionary-based disambiguation strategies. An F-measure of 0.95 could be reached by using the unsupervised approach presented in this paper. The results are promising for a domain-independent abbreviation detection strategy, because our approach avoids retraining of models or use case specific feature engineering efforts required for supervised machine learning approaches.

1 Introduction

Free text narratives are a main carrier of unstructured patient-based information in clinical information systems. Clinical texts differ significantly from, e.g., newspaper or scientific articles. The following snippet demonstrates the high degree of compactness, which is typical for clinical narratives[1]:

```
3.  St.p.  TE eines exulz.  sek.knot.SSM (C43.5) li Lab.
majus.  Level IV, 2,42 mm Tumordurchm.
```

As much as such highly condensed text is understandable by specialists, it poses severe problems to natural language processing (NLP) and subsequent semantic interpretation (Meystre et al., 2008), due to idiosyncrasies of telegram style language like word and term-level ambiguities, acronyms, abbreviations, single-word compounds, derivations, spelling variants and misspellings. In addition, the broad range of clinical specialties with different vocabularies and recording traditions account for a high variation of sub-language characteristics (Patterson et al., 2010).

This paper deals with the disambiguation of the period character (".") in clinical narratives. In many Western languages like German, periods are used as abbreviation markers. Therefore, in a first tokenization step it is not recommended to consider trailing period characters as token delimiters, in order to identify tokens that end with a period. Three cases can be distinguished: (i) The period character marks an abbreviation and does not act as sentence delimiter. (ii) The period character marks an abbreviation and also delimits the sentence. (iii) The period does not belong to the token and therefore delimits the sentence.

---

[1]English translation: "3. History of total excision of an exulcerated secondarily nodular superficially spreading melanoma (C43.5) of the outer left labia. Level 4, tumor diameter 2.42mm".

Proceedings of the Clinical Natural Language Processing Workshop,
pages 91–98, Osaka, Japan, December 11-17 2016.

Our approach is purely data-driven, which distinguishes it from recently published work (Wu et al., 2016; Griffis et al., 2016; Vo et al., 2016), predominantly based on supervised machine learning. In contrast, we avoid extensive manual annotations of training data as well as classification task triggered feature engineering, even though good results were obtained in a previous study (Kreuzthaler and Schulz, 2015). Another requirement is that the method should be easily adaptable to other clinical sub-language domains without model retraining or exhaustive dictionary or terminology management, and that classification results should be understandable in detail and traced back to core decision rules.

2 Materials and Methods

2.1 Data

Corpus: A sample of 1,696 de-identified German-language clinical in and outpatient discharge letters was obtained from the dermatology department of an Austrian university hospital. The documents were randomly assigned to a training and a test corpus, with 848 documents each.

Gold standard: From both corpora a list of word types followed by a period character was extracted by applying the following two regular expression sequentially:
(i) $\b\p{Graph}+\. (?=(\p{Punct}|\s|$))$ matches any word type character sequence ending with a period character, and (ii) $([a-z]+\.|[A-Z][a-z]*\.)$ filters the resulting types from step one by word characters without digits. About 2,300 word types ending with a period finally constitute the training and test set. Their content was manually annotated on whether the period character belongs to the word type or not. The inter-annotator agreement was very high, with a Cohen's kappa of 0.98 (Di Eugenio and Glass, 2004; Hripcsak and Heitjan, 2002).

Dictionary: An abbreviation-free medical dictionary (~1.45 million unique word types) was built using (i) a free contemporary German dictionary[2], (ii) a German medical dictionary (Pschyrembel, 1997), and (iii) texts from a consumer health Web portal[3]. All tokens ending with a period character were excluded from this resource, as a highly sensitive approach to keep it free of abbreviations. In addition, German abbreviations harvested from Web resources[4,5] (~5,800 acronym and abbreviation tokens) were excluded from the overall dictionary to make the final resource as abbreviation-free as possible, also accounting for potential punctuation errors in the three dictionaries such as missing abbreviation period markers. The resulting resource was used in our abbreviation detection strategy, as described in the following section.

2.2 Methods

Statistical approach: For the statistical classification approach we built a fourfold *observed* co-occurrence table $O(k_{nm})$ for every word type ending with a period character:

Schema		Example A		Example B	
Type	¬Type	"Pat"	¬"Pat"	"auf"	¬"auf"
• k_{11}	k_{12}	300	17,970	8	18,262
¬• k_{21}	k_{22}	78	66,718	1,322	65,474

Table 1: Two examples of *observed* corpus based frequency counts, *viz.* the two word types "Pat" and "auf", with and without a period as rightmost character (symbolized by •).

With the observed frequency counts $O(k_{nm})$ we calculate the log-likelihood ratio (LLR) (Dunning, 1993)[6,7] of a word type and its ending period character by use of Shannon's Entropy (Shannon, 1948):

---

[2]http://sourceforge.net/projects/germandict/
[3]http://www.netdoktor.at/
[4]http://de.wikipedia.org/wiki/Medizinische_Abkuerzungen
[5]https://de.wiktionary.org/wiki/Kategorie:Abkuerzung_(Deutsch)
[6]The Apache Mahout library was used for LLR calculation.
[7]http://tdunning.blogspot.co.at/2008/03/surprise-and-coincidence.html

$$H \;=\; -\sum_{i=1}^{n} p_i(log_b p_i) \tag{1}$$

$$LLR \;=\; 2 \cdot N \cdot (H_{matrix} - H_{rows} - H_{cols}) \tag{2}$$

For the cases mentioned in Table 1, LLR values amount to 579.11 for *Example A* and 571.56 for *Example B*. This has the advantage that per co-occurrence their relevance can be asserted assuming a χ^2 distribution (with one degree of freedom) for different significance levels. *Example A* and *Example B* have a very high LLR, which allows the conclusion that the occurrence of the word type left of the ending period character has a *significant* influence on the presence *or* absence of the final period character. In order to determine whether there is significant evidence *for the presence* or *for the absence* of the final period character we calculate, in a next step, the *expected* values $E(k_{nm})$ of the fourfold Table 1 via:

$$k_{11}^{Exp} \;=\; (k_{11} + k_{12}) \cdot (k_{11} + k_{21})/(k_{11} + k_{12} + k_{21} + k_{22}) \tag{3}$$

$$k_{12}^{Exp} \;=\; (k_{12} + k_{11}) \cdot (k_{12} + k_{22})/(k_{11} + k_{12} + k_{21} + k_{22}) \tag{4}$$

$$k_{21}^{Exp} \;=\; (k_{21} + k_{11}) \cdot (k_{21} + k_{22})/(k_{11} + k_{12} + k_{21} + k_{22}) \tag{5}$$

$$k_{22}^{Exp} \;=\; (k_{22} + k_{12}) \cdot (k_{22} + k_{21})/(k_{11} + k_{12} + k_{21} + k_{22}) \tag{6}$$

These equations lead to the following fourfold *expected* co-occurrence table $E(k_{nm})$:

	Schema		Example A		Example B	
	Type	¬Type	"Pat"	¬"Pat"	"auf"	¬"auf"
•	k_{11}^{Exp}	k_{12}^{Exp}	81	18,189	286	17,984
¬•	k_{21}^{Exp}	k_{22}^{Exp}	297	66,499	1,044	65,752

Table 2: Two examples of *expected* corpus based frequency counts, again with the word types "Pat" and "auf", with and without a period as rightmost character (symbolized by •).

The final decision function is now straightforward, reconsidering the fact that the expected values $E(k_{nm})$ can be interpreted as the distribution within the table if there were no divergence from randomness: If $O(k_{11}) - E(k_{11}) > 0$ the period character belongs to the word type and marks an abbreviation, if $O(k_{11}) - E(k_{11}) \leq 0$ the period marker does not belong to it and can be interpreted as sentence delimiter. We apply this decision function regardless of the LLR-level of the token-period co-occurrences, but its influence is inspected in the *Combined approach* described below.

Dictionary approach

The dictionary-based approach for period character classification is done via a simple dictionary lookup of the token under inspection[8]. If the token (without trailing period) is found in the dictionary, we decide that it is not an abbreviation, otherwise the period character is considered as belonging to the token, which is therefore classified as an abbreviation. This strategy requires an abbreviation-free dictionary, as described in Section 2.1.

Combined approach

Our decision function in the combined approach is motivated by the fact that the tokens ending with a period have a distribution pattern as depicted in Figure 1. This has a fundamental influence on our decision function: (i) For a certain proportion of the token-period co-occurrences the statistical approach will have enough frequency information to give valid classification results, (ii) *but* there is a relevant long

---

[8]Due to the large number of about 1.45 million dictionary entries, we used an Apache Lucene index, cf. https://lucene.apache.org/core/

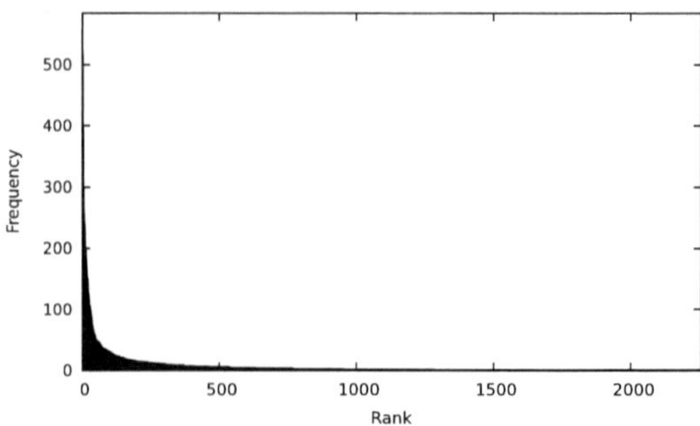

Figure 1: Ranked frequency count of tokens that end with a period.

tail of co-occurrences where the statistical method is not stable any more. We therefore addressed these cases by the dictionary-based approach and to prioritize it in the decision function: wherever the left context of the period is in the dictionary we decide in favor of a non-abbreviation, otherwise we take the decision of the statistical approach taking into account different significance levels ($LLR_1 > 10.83, p < 0.001$; $LLR_2 > 3.84, p < 0.05$; $LLR_3 > 0, p$-value not considered).

> **if** *token* $\exists$ *dictionary* **then**
> $\quad | \quad \rightarrow$ abbr=false;
> **else if** $LLR >$ *significance level* **then**
> $\quad\quad$ **if** $O(k_{11}) - E(k_{11}) > 0$ **then**
> $\quad\quad | \quad \rightarrow$ abbr=true;
> $\quad\quad$ **else**
> $\quad\quad | \quad \rightarrow$ abbr=false;
> $\quad\quad$ **end**
> **else**
> $\quad | \quad \rightarrow$ abbr=true
> **end**

Algorithm 1: Combined decision algorithm.

3 Results and Discussion

The evaluation results show that the *Statistical approach* on its own tends to find all abbreviations but lacks precision. The *Dictionary approach* returns an F-measure of 0.94, and the top performance result of $F_1 = 0.95$ is obtained with the combined approach. The evaluation results of the *Combined approach* also reflect the fact that the LLR information can be neglected in that case and the outcome of $O(k_{11}) - E(k_{11})$ should always be used regardless of the impact of the significance of the token-period co-occurrence. The investigation of false positives shows, e.g., a noticeable amount of token-period co-occurrences like "Lymphknotenstatus." (in English "lymph node status.") which very commonly appear at the end of a sentence, but which are not in our dictionary (search term: "Lymphknotenstatus"), and have a $O(k_{11}) - E(k_{11}) > 0$. False negative results typically appear with abbreviated tokens, such as "morph." (abbreviation for "morphologisch", in English "morphological"), which are erroneously found in our dictionary (search term: "morph") and are therefore classified as non-abbreviations.

Kiss and Strunk (2002a), tried to reduce the amount of false positives and false negatives by applying different scaling factors to the resulting LLR. A final threshold was manually chosen, with F-measures of 0.92 and higher on newspaper corpora. Kiss and Strunk (2002b) performed an intermediate evaluation of their idea of re-scaling the LLR also for sentence boundary detection. Here, they obtained a minimum F-measure of 0.91. Both preliminary approaches finally led to the *Punkt* system (Kiss and Strunk, 2006), a multilingual unsupervised approach rigorously tested and evaluated. Kreuzthaler and Schulz (2014) applied an extended version of the Kiss and Strunk (2002a) method in an initial experiment with clinical

| | Training | | | Test | | |
Method	Precision	Recall	F_1	Precision	Recall	F_1
Statistical						
Token	0.47	1.00	0.64	0.44	1.00	0.61
Type	0.36	0.97	0.53	0.35	0.97	0.51
Dictionary						
Token	0.90	0.98	0.94	0.88	0.97	0.93
Type	0.57	0.81	0.67	0.54	0.80	0.65
Combined$_{LLR_1}$						
Token	0.91	0.98	0.94	0.89	0.97	0.93
Type	0.57	0.81	0.67	0.56	0.80	0.66
Combined$_{LLR_2}$						
Token	0.92	0.97	0.94	0.90	0.97	0.94
Type	0.58	0.80	0.67	0.56	0.79	0.66
Combined$_{LLR_3}$						
Token	0.94	0.97	**0.95**	0.92	0.97	**0.94**
Type	0.61	0.78	0.69	0.59	0.78	0.67

Table 3: Evaluation results.

texts and achieved an accuracy of 0.93 for abbreviation and sentence detection based on the interpretation of the period character. A supervised machine learning approach using a support vector machine with a linear kernel and thorough feature engineering led to an F-measure of 0.95 for abbreviation detection and an F-measure 0.94 for sentence delineation (Kreuzthaler and Schulz, 2015).

Studies have also focused on the detection, normalization, and context-dependent mapping of abbreviations/acronyms to long forms (Xu et al., 2012). This is also part of works such as CLEF 2013 (Suominen et al., 2013), which included a task for acronym/abbreviation normalization, using the UMLS[9] as target terminology. An F-measure of 0.89 was reported by Patrick et al. (2013). Four different methods for abbreviation detection were tested by Xu et al. (2007). A decision tree classifier, which additionally used features from knowledge resources, performed best with a precision of 0.91 and a recall of 0.80. Wu et al. (2011) compared machine learning methods for abbreviation detection. Word formation, vowel combinations, related content from knowledge bases, word frequency in the overall corpus, and local context were used as features. A random forest classifier performed best with an F-measure of 0.95 and an ensemble of classifiers achieved the highest F-measure of 0.96. Wu et al. (2012) compared different clinical natural language processing systems for abbreviation handling in clinical narratives: MedLEE (Friedman et al., 1995b; Friedman et al., 1995a) performed best with an F-Measure of 0.60. A prototypical system, meeting real-time constraints, is described in Wu et al. (2013). Wu's journey finally ended in the CARD system (Wu et al., 2016) achieving an F-measure of 0.76 for finding *and* disambiguating abbreviations in clinical narratives. Very recently Vo et al. (2016) got very high results with a minimum F-measure of 0.94 on abbreviation detection on clinical notes applying supervised machine learning methods which a rich feature engineering process.

The main difference between the work we presented and the unsupervised approach of Kiss and Strunk is the fact that we refrained from re-scaling the LLR and avoided to set an experimental threshold for the abbreviation classification task. The statistical decision function we employed proved to be solid and robust even in cases where $k_{21} > k_{11}$ (e.g. "Meta." with $k_{11} = 28$, $k_{21} = 82$, but nevertheless correctly classified as abbreviation), which had also been one type of motivation for introducing scaling factors by Kiss and Strunk (2006). In contrast to much of the related work, our approach is unsupervised

---

[9]http://www.nlm.nih.gov/research/umls/

and does not require the training of a machine learning model or a rich feature engineering effort (Vo et al., 2016; Wu et al., 2016; Kreuzthaler and Schulz, 2015). Therefore we hypothesize that our approach is especially suited to be deployed to other clinical domains, which was a main driver of our investigations. Table 3 shows that with the dictionary approach alone we got F-measure values greater than 0.93, whereas the performance by word types was much lower. For the time being, we consider this acceptable because we concentrate on high token-based evaluation measurements and do not want to misclassify frequently occurring abbreviations. The statistical approach is not applicable in isolation, because we have found many cases where a word type followed by a period occurs only once or twice in the corpus (see Figure 1). In such cases the statistical approach is not robust any longer, so we have to rely on dictionaries. The combined approach was satisfactory as both training and test yielded token-based F-measure values for period character disambiguation greater than 0.94.

4 Conclusion and Outlook

In this paper we presented an unsupervised approach for period character disambiguation in German clinical narratives, which we evaluated for the task of abbreviation detection. We motivated and introduced both a data-driven statistical approach and a dictionary-based method. Based on the analysis of the frequency distribution of token-period character co-occurrences we also presented a hybrid methodology. This hybrid approach put emphasis on the dictionary-based method, which was then supported by a statistical decision rule. A dermatology corpus was used for initial evaluation. For the training and test set, we obtained F-measures of 0.95 and 0.94, respectively. This supports the hypothesis that unsupervised approaches are well suited for abbreviation and sentence boundary detection in clinical narratives, which are known to abound with ad-hoc abbreviations. Furthermore, the system presented here needs no adjustment to the sublanguage, which makes it easy to reuse for other text genres and subject-matters. This consideration together with the ability to trace back decision results to their core classification logic and the avoidance of manual training data annotations were major drivers for this investigation.

We mention the following limitations: (i) Periods after digits are currently not considered despite their importance as markers of ordinals in many languages, as well as their importance in many data formats. Kreuzthaler and Schulz (2015) took this into account in a supervised rich feature engineering approach using support vector machines; (ii) The methodology presented in this paper cannot resolve cases where periods play a double role, *viz.* as both abbreviation markers and sentence delimiters. This can be addressed by including in-depth context information regarding the period character under investigation; (iii) We applied this method to only one kind of text, *viz.* medical discharge summaries of melanoma patients. Therefore, we plan to demonstrate domain independence by applying the same approach to cardiology reports; (iv) We only used German texts, so that we can say little about the generalizability to other languages. Although we have found that ad hoc abbreviation is a very common phenomenon also in other languages and text genres, it cannot always be taken for granted that the period character is used as a marker. Future investigations will address these problems. Our goal is to create a specific UIMA component for abbreviation detection and resolution with an unsupervised core, which could be integrated in a clinical NLP pipeline like cTAKES (Savova et al., 2010), The Leo framework - The VINCI-developed NLP infrastructure (Meystre et al., 2008; Patterson et al., 2014) or MedKATp.

Acknowledgements

This work has been carried out as part of the IICCAB project (Innovative Use of Information for Clinical Care and Biomarker Research) within the K1 COMET Competence Center CBmed, which is funded by the Austrian Federal Ministry of Transport, Innovation and Technology (BMVIT); the Austrian Federal Ministry of Science, Research and Economy (BMWFW); the Austrian state of Styria (Department 12, Business and Innovation); the Styrian Business Promotion Agency (SFG); and the Vienna Business Agency.

References

Barbara Di Eugenio and Michael Glass. 2004. The kappa statistic: A second look. *Computational Linguistics*, 30(1):95–101.

Ted Dunning. 1993. Accurate methods for the statistics of surprise and coincidence. *Computational Linguistics*, 19(1):61–74.

Carol Friedman, George Hripcsak, William DuMouchel, Stephen B Johnson, and Paul D Clayton. 1995a. Natural language processing in an operational clinical information system. *Natural Language Engineering*, 1(01):83–108.

Carol Friedman, Stephen B Johnson, Bruce Forman, and Justin Starren. 1995b. Architectural requirements for a multipurpose natural language processor in the clinical environment. In *Proceedings of the Annual Symposium on Computer Application in Medical Care*, pages 347–351. American Medical Informatics Association.

Denis Griffis, Chaitanya Shivade, Eric Fosler-Lussier, and Albert M Lai. 2016. A quantitative and qualitative evaluation of sentence boundary detection for the clinical domain. *AMIA Summits on Translational Science Proceedings*, 2016:88–97.

George Hripcsak and Daniel F Heitjan. 2002. Measuring agreement in medical informatics reliability studies. *Journal of Biomedical Informatics*, 35(2):99–110.

Tibor Kiss and Jan Strunk. 2002a. Scaled log likelihood ratios for the detection of abbreviations in text corpora. In *Proceedings of the 19th International Conference on Computational Linguistics-Volume 2*, pages 1–5. Association for Computational Linguistics.

Tibor Kiss and Jan Strunk. 2002b. Viewing sentence boundary detection as collocation identification. *Proceedings of KONVENS 2002*, pages 75–82.

Tibor Kiss and Jan Strunk. 2006. Unsupervised multilingual sentence boundary detection. *Computational Linguistics*, 32(4):485–525.

Markus Kreuzthaler and Stefan Schulz. 2014. Disambiguation of period characters in clinical narratives. In *Proceedings of the 5th International Workshop on Health Text Mining and Information Analysis (Louhi)@EACL*, volume 100, pages 96–100.

Markus Kreuzthaler and Stefan Schulz. 2015. Detection of sentence boundaries and abbreviations in clinical narratives. *BMC Medical Informatics and Decision Making*, 15(2):1–13.

Stéphane M Meystre, Guergana K Savova, Karin C Kipper-Schuler, John F Hurdle, et al. 2008. Extracting information from textual documents in the electronic health record: a review of recent research. *Yearb Med Inform*, 35:128–44.

Jon D Patrick, Leila Safari, and Ying Ou. 2013. ShARe/CLEF eHealth 2013 Normalization of Acronyms/Abbreviations Challenge. In *CLEF 2013 Evaluation Labs and Workshop Abstracts - Working Notes*.

Olga Patterson, Sean Igo, and John F Hurdle. 2010. Automatic acquisition of sublanguage semantic schema: Towards the word sense disambiguation of clinical narratives. In *AMIA Annual Symposium Proceedings*, volume 2010, pages 612–616. American Medical Informatics Association.

OV Patterson, TB Forbush, SD Saini, SE Moser, and SL DuVall. 2014. Classifying the indication for colonoscopy procedures: A comparison of NLP approaches in a diverse national healthcare system. *Studies in Health Technology and Informatics*, 216:614–618.

Pschyrembel. 1997. Klinisches Wörterbuch. CD-ROM Version 1/97.

Guergana K Savova, James J Masanz, Philip V Ogren, Jiaping Zheng, Sunghwan Sohn, Karin C Kipper-Schuler, and Christopher G Chute. 2010. Mayo clinical Text Analysis and Knowledge Extraction System (cTAKES): architecture, component evaluation and applications. *Journal of the American Medical Informatics Association*, 17(5):507–513.

Claude Elwood Shannon. 1948. A mathematical theory of communication. *The Bell System Technical Journal*, 27:379–423, 623–656.

Hanna Suominen, Sanna Salanterä, Sumithra Velupillai, Wendy W Chapman, Guergana Savova, Noemie Elhadad, Sameer Pradhan, Brett R South, Danielle L Mowery, Gareth JF Jones, et al. 2013. Overview of the ShARe/CLEF eHealth Evaluation Lab 2013. In *International Conference of the Cross-Language Evaluation Forum for European Languages*, pages 212–231. Springer.

Thi Ngoc Chau Vo, Tru Hoang Cao, and Tu Bao Ho. 2016. Abbreviation identification in clinical notes with level-wise feature engineering and supervised learning. In *Pacific Rim Knowledge Acquisition Workshop*, pages 3–17. Springer.

Yonghui Wu, S Trent Rosenbloom, Joshua C Denny, Randolph A Miller, Subramani Mani, Dario A Giuse, and Hua Xu. 2011. Detecting abbreviations in discharge summaries using machine learning methods. In *AMIA Annual Symposium Proceedings*, volume 2011, pages 1541–1549.

Yonghui Wu, Joshua C Denny, Samuel Rosenbloom, Randolph A Miller, Dario A Giuse, and Hua Xu. 2012. A comparative study of current clinical natural language processing systems on handling abbreviations in discharge summaries. In *AMIA Annual Symposium Proceedings*, volume 2012, pages 997–1003.

Yonghui Wu, Joshua Denny, S Trent Rosenbloom, Randolph A Miller, Dario A Giuse, Min Song, and Hua Xu. 2013. A prototype application for real-time recognition and disambiguation of clinical abbreviations. In *Proceedings of the 7th International Workshop on Data and Text Mining in Biomedical Informatics*, pages 7–8.

Yonghui Wu, Joshua C Denny, S Trent Rosenbloom, Randolph A Miller, Dario A Giuse, Lulu Wang, Carmelo Blanquicett, Ergin Soysal, Jun Xu, and Hua Xu. 2016. A long journey to short abbreviations: developing an open-source framework for clinical abbreviation recognition and disambiguation (CARD). *Journal of the American Medical Informatics Association*, page ocw109.

Hua Xu, Peter D Stetson, and Carol Friedman. 2007. A study of abbreviations in clinical notes. In *AMIA Annual Symposium Proceedings*, volume 2007, pages 821–825.

Hua Xu, Peter D Stetson, and Carol Friedman. 2012. Combining corpus-derived sense profiles with estimated frequency information to disambiguate clinical abbreviations. In *AMIA Annual Symposium Proceedings*, volume 2012, pages 1004–1013.

Automated Anonymization as Spelling Variant Detection

Steven Kester Yuwono   **Hwee Tou Ng**
Department of Computer Science
National University of Singapore
13 Computing Drive
Singapore 117417
{kester,nght}@comp.nus.edu.sg

Kee Yuan Ngiam
Department of Surgery
National University Hospital
5 Lower Kent Ridge Road
Singapore 119074
kee_yuan_ngiam@nuhs.edu.sg

Abstract

The issue of privacy has always been a concern when clinical texts are used for research purposes. Personal health information (PHI) (such as name and identification number) needs to be removed so that patients cannot be identified. Manual anonymization is not feasible due to the large number of clinical texts to be anonymized. In this paper, we tackle the task of anonymizing clinical texts written in sentence fragments and which frequently contain symbols, abbreviations, and misspelled words. Our clinical texts therefore differ from those in the i2b2 shared tasks which are in prose form with complete sentences. Our clinical texts are also part of a structured database which contains patient name and identification number in structured fields. As such, we formulate our anonymization task as spelling variant detection, exploiting patients' personal information in the structured fields to detect their spelling variants in clinical texts. We successfully anonymized clinical texts consisting of more than 200 million words, using minimum edit distance and regular expression patterns.

1 Introduction

Clinical discharge summaries are an essential source of information to facilitate medical research. However, they contain patients' personal health information (PHI) which, if disclosed, would compromise patients' privacy. Various techniques have been applied to create de-identification systems and they have performed well (Uzuner et al., 2007). These de-identifier systems utilize either machine learning approaches such as support vector machines (Uzuner et al., 2008), conditional random fields (Wellner et al., 2007), and decision trees (Szarvas et al., 2007), or rule-based approaches with pattern matching (Douglass et al., 2004).

In this paper, we tackle the task of anonymizing clinical discharge summaries written in English from the National University Hospital in Singapore. Our work is novel in the following aspects: (1) Our clinical discharge summaries are written in sentence fragments and they frequently contain symbols, abbreviations, and misspelled words, unlike the clinical texts in the i2b2 shared tasks which are in prose form with complete sentences. (2) We treat anonymization as a spelling variant detection task, by exploiting patient health information stored in structured fields. (3) We have applied our anonymization algorithm on actual hospital discharge summaries containing more than 200 million words. Manual evaluation on a sample test set shows that our algorithm achieves very high recall.

2 Task Description

The corpus of hospital discharge summaries used in this paper is obtained from the National University Hospital, spanning a period of ten years. The patients in these discharge summaries came from a variety of countries with varied names from different races and cultures. In all, there are about 570,000 discharge summaries with a total size of more than 700MB. Each discharge summary has an average of 400 word tokens. Given a discharge summary, the anonymization task is to remove patients' PHI which includes the following items: names of patients; identification numbers; telephone, fax, and pager numbers;

Proceedings of the Clinical Natural Language Processing Workshop,
pages 99–103, Osaka, Japan, December 11-17 2016.

geographical locations; dates; and names of doctors and hospitals. It is highly improbable that a patient can be identified without the personal information listed above. Any PHI detected will be replaced by an appropriate surrogate, e.g., a patient name will be replaced by PNAME, a patient identification number will be replaced by PID, etc.

As mentioned earlier, our discharge summaries are written in sentence fragments and organized in bullet points. They frequently contain symbols, abbreviations, and misspelled words. As such, our discharge summaries are significantly different from those in the i2b2 shared tasks in 2006 (Uzuner et al., 2007) and 2014 (Stubbs et al., 2015), which are in prose form with complete sentences. Samples of discharge summaries from our corpus and from the i2b2 shared task in 2006 are given below.

```
This 68 year old female had rheumatic
    fever in the past , and has had
    chronic atrial fibrillation .
She has had progressive heart failure
    and an evaluation demonstrated
    worsening mitral stenosis with
    severe pulmonary hypertension .
Because of her deteriorating status ,
    she underwent prior cardiac
    catheterization , which confirmed
    severe mitral stenosis with
    secondary tricuspid valve
    regurgitation due to pulmonary
    hypertension .
She was referred for valve surgery .
She had undergone a previous nasal
    arterial embolization for treatment
    of recurrent epistaxis .
She had a partial gastrectomy in 1972 .
Her MEDICATIONS ON ADMISSION included
    Coumadin , digoxin , 0.125 , qD ,
    Lasix , 40 , q.i.d. , and Vanceril
    inhaler .
```

```
33/Chinese/M
PMHX:
- anemia
- previously on iron supplement
- nil OGD done

Currently c/o:
epigastric pain 1500H
nil nasuea / vomiting
nil fever noted
nil dysuria / hematuria
no changes in bowel movement
no LOW/LOA
no chest pain or SOB

O/E on admission:
Pt alert, attentive
CVS: PR 78/min, Bp 120/70 S1S2 no
    murmurs, TWC 14 UC10 - nad
soft abdo, normoactivew BS. direct and
    rebound tenderness RIF. nil guarding
    . nil rebound

Imperssion: Acute appendicitis
Pt was sent for op
```

A sample discharge summary snippet from the i2b2 de-identification challenge in 2006.

A sample discharge summary snippet from our hospital.

In our discharge summary snippet above, the words nasuea and Imperssion are misspelled words. Pt, PMHX, LOW, and LOA are abbreviations for patient, past medical history, loss of weight, and loss of appetite respectively. As such, our discharge summaries pose additional challenges to anonymization and to subsequent processing by downstream natural language processing modules like part-of-speech tagging, coreference resolution, etc.

In addition, our hospital discharge summaries are part of a structured database which contains patients' PHI such as names, identification numbers, phone numbers, etc. in structured fields. As such, we exploit the meta-data in these structured fields and formulate our anonymization task as spelling variant detection. That is, the objective of our anonymization task is to find spelling variants of patient names and other PHI items and replace them with appropriate anonymized surrogates. This is in contrast to the i2b2 shared tasks, where external structured information is not utilized. Since hospitals are required to keep track of patients' PHI in addition to their discharge summaries, admission notes, etc, one can expect structured PHI items of a patient to be available in a real-world setting when processing the discharge summary of a patient. As such, the anonymization task that we address is a more realistic one.

3 Anonymization Algorithm

Our anonymization algorithm uses regular expression matching and the minimum edit distance algorithm to identify spelling variants, assuming that patients' PHI stored in the structured database is correct.

3.1 Patient Name

Patient name is the most important personal information present in a discharge summary. Even a misspelled patient name may be used to trace and identify a patient. A patient's full name associated with a discharge summary is first taken from the structured field in the database. The full name is first split into individual name tokens. Each word in a discharge summary is compared against each name token of the patient. The minimum edit distance algorithm (Wagner and Fischer, 1974) is used to compute the minimum edit distance between a name token n from the structured field and a candidate word w in the discharge summary. We set the insertion, deletion, and replacement cost to 1. The edit distance ratio R is computed as $\frac{d}{min(|n|,|w|)}$, where d is the minimum edit distance of n and w. Since a longer name has a higher probability of being misspelled than a shorter one, we use R to take into account the length of a string. If R is less than a specified threshold, the current candidate word w will be taken as the patient's name, and will be anonymized and replaced by a surrogate. We set the threshold to be 0.33.

A person's name is often preceded by an honorific (a title prefixing a person's name). As such, we replace the word after an honorific by a surrogate. The list of honorifics used in our anonymization algorithm is as follows: `mr, mrs, miss, ms, madam, mdm, lady, sir, col, dr, doctor, a/prof, e/prof, professor, prof, general, gen, senator, sen.` By detecting the honorifics, our anonymization algorithm is able to detect names that might otherwise be missed by the minimum edit distance algorithm.

3.2 Identification Number and Contact Number

To detect a patient's identification number and contact numbers, we make use of regular expressions that capture the generic formats of patients' identification numbers and contact numbers. The format of patient identification numbers in our hospital consists of fixed numbers of letters and digits arranged in a fixed order, which can be readily detected by a regular expression. Similarly, the format of contact numbers consists of digits interspersed with space or dash ("-") characters, which again can be readily detected by a regular expression.

3.3 Date

Anonymization of dates is challenging because there are many possible date formats. Days can be written in single or double-digit. Months can be written in single-digit, double-digit, short name (e.g., Jan), or long name (e.g., January). Years can be written in double-digit or four-digit. The delimiters allowed between day, month, and year include dash (-), comma (,), slash (/), colon (:), and white space (space and tab). Therefore we have created regular expressions for all possible combinations of the date format to cover all possibilities: day/month/year, month/day/year, year/day/month, year/month/day, day/month, month/day, year/month, and month/year.

3.4 Doctor's Name, Hospital's Name, and Geographical Location

Most doctors' names are handled by patient name anonymization above due to the common occurrences of "dr" or "prof" preceding a doctor's name. In addition, we obtain a list of names of doctors, hospitals, and geographical locations in Singapore. For each entry in the list, we check if it is present in a discharge summary and replace it by a surrogate if found.

4 Evaluation

One key advantage of our anonymization algorithm that relies on regular expression matching and the minimum edit distance algorithm is that manual annotation of training data is *not* required, unlike in a machine learning approach. To evaluate the performance of our anonymization algorithm, 100 discharge summaries were randomly selected as the test set. The accuracy of our anonymization algorithm is reported in Table 1.

---

[1]Patients' identification numbers and contact numbers
[2]Names of doctors, hospitals, and geographical locations

	Patient name	ID num[1]	Date	Other names[2]	Overall
Recall	100	100	100	93.14	97.35
Precision	85.94	100	66.03	76.71	72.67
F1-score	92.44	100	79.50	84.13	83.22
PHI count	110	29	418	350	907

Table 1: Token-level evaluation of our anonymization algorithm (in %).

Our anonymization algorithm has achieved good performance. In particular, it achieves 100% recall on anonymizing patients' names, identification numbers, and contact numbers. We favor recall over precision, since it is highly critical that personal information of patients be completely anonymized, at the cost of some false positives. The anonymization algorithm fails to detect some other names, such as doctors' names which are not present in the given list of doctors' names. Most of the false positives are contributed by some common names of doctors, and how time duration is written in the discharge summaries. To illustrate, consider the following sentence fragment: `vomiting 2/7, LOW 1/12.` `2/7` is falsely detected as a date (meaning 2 days). `1/12` is falsely detected as a date (meaning 1 month). `LOW` is falsely detected as a doctor's name, because `LOW` is a common family name in Singapore.

Our anonymization algorithm runs efficiently. It anonymizes 7 discharge summaries per second, and takes 21.7 hours to anonymize the whole corpus of discharge summaries consisting of more than 200 million words on a PC with 3.4 GHz processor in a single thread.

We have also attempted to use a machine learning approach, in particular a maximum entropy classifier, to carry out anonymization. The classifier uses the edit distance ratio as the main feature, and other additional features such as part-of-speech tags, named entity tags, binary features about the presence of a preceding honorific and whether the current word is an English word. However, preliminary experiments indicate that the maximum entropy classifier does not outperform our current anonymization algorithm of regular expression matching and the minimum edit distance algorithm. As such, we adopt our current algorithm which is simpler and requires no annotated training data.

There were several prior systems which focused on the detection or removal of certain types of PHI such as patient names (Taira et al., 2002), or both patient and doctor names (Thomas et al., 2002). However, they did not exploit knowledge of external structured information like patient names or other PHI to be removed. There were also several studies that used patients' structured fields to perform de-identification using regular expressions and lexical look-up tables (Neamatullah et al., 2008), string similarity algorithm to detect typographical errors (Friedlin and McDonald, 2008), and a combination of rule-based and machine learning approaches for de-identification (Ferrández et al., 2013). However, the performance of these systems cannot be directly compared to ours because of different test data.

5   Conclusion

In this paper, we tackle the task of anonymizing discharge summaries written in sentence fragments and which frequently contain symbols, abbreviations, and misspelled words. Our discharge summaries are therefore substantially different from the discharge summaries dealt with in the i2b2 shared tasks. We also exploit PHI of patients present in structured database fields and present a novel approach that treats anonymization as spelling variant detection. Our anonymization algorithm effectively and efficiently anonymizes more than 200 million words of actual hospital discharge summaries, achieving a very high recall.

Acknowledgments

This research is supported by Singapore Ministry of Education Academic Research Fund Tier 1 grant T1-251RES1513.

References

M Douglass, GD Clifford, A Reisner, GB Moody, and RG Mark. 2004. Computer-assisted de-identification of free text in the MIMIC II database. In *Computers in Cardiology 2004*, pages 341–344.

Oscar Ferrández, Brett R South, Shuying Shen, F Jeffrey Friedlin, Matthew H Samore, and Stéphane M Meystre. 2013. BoB, a best-of-breed automated text de-identification system for VHA clinical documents. *Journal of the American Medical Informatics Association*, 20(1):77–83.

F Jeff Friedlin and Clement J McDonald. 2008. A software tool for removing patient identifying information from clinical documents. *Journal of the American Medical Informatics Association*, 15(5):601–610.

Ishna Neamatullah, Margaret M Douglass, Li-wei H Lehman, Andrew Reisner, Mauricio Villarroel, William J Long, Peter Szolovits, George B Moody, Roger G Mark, and Gari D Clifford. 2008. Automated de-identification of free-text medical records. *BMC Medical Informatics and Decision Making*, 8:32.

Amber Stubbs, Christopher Kotfila, and Özlem Uzuner. 2015. Automated systems for the de-identification of longitudinal clinical narratives: Overview of 2014 i2b2/UTHealth shared task track 1. *Journal of Biomedical Informatics*, 58:S11–S19.

György Szarvas, Richárd Farkas, and Róbert Busa-Fekete. 2007. State-of-the-art anonymization of medical records using an iterative machine learning framework. *Journal of the American Medical Informatics Association*, 14(5):574–580.

Ricky K Taira, Alex AT Bui, and Hooshang Kangarloo. 2002. Identification of patient name references within medical documents using semantic selectional restrictions. In *Proceedings of the AMIA Symposium*, page 757.

Sean M Thomas, Burke Mamlin, Gunther Schadow, and Clement McDonald. 2002. A successful technique for removing names in pathology reports using an augmented search and replace method. In *Proceedings of the AMIA Symposium*, page 777.

Özlem Uzuner, Yuan Luo, and Peter Szolovits. 2007. Evaluating the state-of-the-art in automatic de-identification. *Journal of the American Medical Informatics Association*, 14(5):550–563.

Özlem Uzuner, Tawanda C Sibanda, Yuan Luo, and Peter Szolovits. 2008. A de-identifier for medical discharge summaries. *Artificial intelligence in Medicine*, 42(1):13–35.

R. A. Wagner and M. J. Fischer. 1974. The string-to-string correction problem. *Journal of the Association for Computing Machinery*, 21:168–173.

Ben Wellner, Matt Huyck, Scott Mardis, John Aberdeen, Alex Morgan, Leonid Peshkin, Alex Yeh, Janet Hitzeman, and Lynette Hirschman. 2007. Rapidly retargetable approaches to de-identification in medical records. *Journal of the American Medical Informatics Association*, 14(5):564–573.

Author Index

Association for Computational Linguistics
209 N. Eighth Street
Stroudsburg, Pennsylvania 18360